Life Lessons
from THE INSPIRED WORD of GOD

BOOKS of
EZRA & NEHEMIAH

MAX LUCADO
General Editor

TABLE OF CONTENTS

HOW TO STUDY THE BIBLE

BY MAX LUCADO

This is a peculiar book you are holding. Words crafted in another language. Deeds done in a distant era. Events recorded in a far-off land. Counsel offered to a foreign people. This is a peculiar book.

It's surprising that anyone reads it. It's too old. Some of its writings date back five thousand years. It's too bizarre. The book speaks of incredible floods, fires, earthquakes, and people with supernatural abilities. It's too radical. The Bible calls for undying devotion to a carpenter who called himself God's Son.

Logic says this book shouldn't survive. Too old, too bizarre, too radical.

The Bible has been banned, burned, scoffed, and ridiculed. Scholars have mocked it as foolish. Kings have branded it as illegal. A thousand times over it the grave has been dug and the dirge has begun, but somehow the Bible never stays in the grave. Not only has it survived, it has thrived. It is the single most popular book in all of history. It has been the best-selling book in the world for years!

There is no way on earth to explain it. Which perhaps is the only explanation. The answer? The Bible's durability is not found on earth; it is found in heaven. For the millions who have tested its claims and claimed its promises, there is but one answer—the Bible is God's book and God's voice.

As you read it, you would be wise to give some thought to two questions. What is the purpose of the Bible? and How do I study the Bible? Time spent reflecting on these two issues will greatly enhance your Bible study.

What is the purpose of the Bible?

Let the Bible itself answer that question.

Since you were a child you have known the Holy Scriptures which are able to make you wise. And that wisdom leads to salvation through faith in Christ Jesus.

(2 Tim. 3:15)

The purpose of the Bible? Salvation. God's highest passion is to get his children home. His book, the Bible, describes his plan of salvation. The purpose of the Bible is to proclaim God's plan and passion to save his children.

That is the reason this book has endured through the centuries. It dares to tackle the toughest questions about life: Where do I go after I die? Is there a God? What do I do with my fears? The Bible offers answers to these crucial questions. It is the treasure map that leads us to God's highest treasure, eternal life.

But how do we use the Bible? Countless copies of Scripture sit unread on bookshelves and nightstands simply because people don't know how to read it. What can we do to make the Bible real in our lives?

The clearest answer is found in the words of Jesus.

"Ask," he promised, *"and God will give to you. Search, and you will find. Knock, and the door will open for you."*

(Matt. 7:7)

The first step in understanding the Bible is asking God to help us. We should read prayerfully. If anyone understands God's Word, it is because of God and not the reader.

But the Helper will teach you everything and will cause you to remember all that I told you. The Helper is the Holy Spirit whom the Father will send in my name.

(John 14:26)

Before reading the Bible, pray. Invite God to speak to you. Don't go to Scripture looking for your idea, go searching for his.

Not only should we read the Bible prayerfully, we should read it carefully. *Search and you will find* is the pledge. The Bible is not a newspaper to be skimmed but rather a mine to be quarried. *Search for it like silver, and hunt for it like hidden treasure. Then you will understand respect for the LORD, and you will find that you know God* (Prov. 2:4).

Any worthy find requires effort. The Bible is no exception. To understand the Bible you don't have to be brilliant, but you must be willing to roll up your sleeves and search.

Be a worker who is not ashamed and who uses the true teaching in the right way.

(2 Tim. 2:15)

Here's a practical point. Study the Bible a bit at a time. Hunger is not satisfied by eating twenty-one meals in one sitting once a week. The body needs a steady diet to remain strong. So does the soul. When God sent food to his people in the wilderness, he didn't provide loaves already made. Instead, he sent them manna in the shape of *thin flakes like frost . . . on the desert ground* (Exod. 16:14).

God gave manna in limited portions.

God sends spiritual food the same way. He opens the heavens with just enough nutrients for today's hunger. He provides, *a command here, a command there. A rule here, a rule there. A little lesson here, a little lesson there* (Isa. 28:10).

Don't be discouraged if your reading reaps a small harvest. Some days a lesser portion is all that is needed. What is important is to search every day for that day's message. A steady diet of God's Word over a lifetime builds a healthy soul and mind.

A little girl returned from her first day at school. Her mom asked, "Did you learn anything?" "Apparently not enough," the girl responded, "I have to go back tomorrow and the next day and the next. . . ."

Such is the case with learning. And such is the case with Bible study. Understanding comes little by little over a lifetime.

There is a third step in understanding the Bible. After the asking and seeking comes the knocking. After you ask and search, then knock.

Knock, and the door will open for you.
(Matt. 7:7)

To knock is to stand at God's door. To make yourself available. To climb the steps, cross the porch, stand at the doorway, and volunteer. Knocking goes beyond the realm of thinking and into the realm of acting.

To knock is to ask, What can I do? How can I obey? Where can I go?

It's one thing to know what to do. It's another to do it. But for those who do it, those who choose to obey, a special reward awaits them.

The truly happy are those who carefully study God's perfect law that makes people free, and they continue to study it. They do not forget what they heard, but they obey what God's teaching says. Those who do this will be made happy.

(James 1:25)

What a promise. Happiness comes to those who do what they read! It's the same with medicine. If you only read the label but ignore the pills, it won't help. It's the same with food. If you only read the recipe but never cook, you won't be fed. And it's the same with the Bible. If you only read the words but never obey, you'll never know the joy God has promised.

Ask. Search. Knock. Simple, isn't it? Why don't you give it a try? If you do, you'll see why you are holding the most remarkable book in history.

EZRA

INTRODUCTION

Martin Luther you've heard of. Philipp Melanchthon, probably not. But Luther knew Melanchthon. And Luther was a better man as a result.

Melanchthon was the intellectual of the Reformation. He authored the Augsburg Confession. He was the first to put into writing an evangelical theology.

He was only eleven when his father died, only twelve when his grandfather presented him with a Bible and a Greek grammar. The next fifty years the three were inseparable. Melanchthon's one great love was to teach the Word of God.

He didn't just read the Bible, he devoured it. By the age of seventeen he was a faculty member at the University of Wittenberg. Though he was small of frame and frail of health, he was keen of mind.

And even more important, he was keen of purpose.

He lived to study and teach the Bible. He commanded the respect of Martin Luther. "I was born to fight," he said, "but Master Philip, he comes along sowing with joy."

The prophet Ezra was the Philip Melanchthon of his day. Ezra was the second of three key leaders to leave Babylon for the reconstruction of Jerusalem. Zerubbabel was first. Then Ezra and then Nehemiah. Zerubbabel reconstructed the Temple, Nehemiah rebuilt the walls, and Ezra restored the worship.

Any person who has tackled the task of presenting the Bible to people will find a friend in Ezra. He was a student. He was an interpreter. In fact, the clearest Old Testament reference to exposition is attributed to Ezra. He was the head of the Levites who "read from the Book of the Teachings of God and explained what it meant so the people understood what was being read" (Nehemiah 8:8).

Don't you appreciate that last phrase, "and explained what it meant so the people understood . . ."? Don't you appreciate the person who can take the Word and reveal it for your life?

Perhaps you can do that. If so, stay faithful. There is no higher task. Perhaps you have a teacher like that. If so, be grateful. There is no greater friend.

LESSON ONE

OBEYING GOD'S CALL

REFLECTION

Begin your study by sharing thoughts on this question.

1. Think of a time when you obeyed God's call to do something. What blessings did you experience as a result of your obedience?

_____

_____

_____

BIBLE READING

Read Ezra 1:1–11 from the NCV or the NKJV.

NCV

¹In the first year Cyrus was king of Persia, the LORD caused Cyrus to send an announcement to his whole kingdom and to put it in writing. This happened so the LORD's message spoken by Jeremiah would come true. He wrote:

²This is what Cyrus king of Persia says:
The LORD, the God of heaven, has given all the kingdoms of the earth to me, and he

NKJV

¹Now in the first year of Cyrus king of Persia, that the word of the LORD by the mouth of Jeremiah might be fulfilled, the LORD stirred up the spirit of Cyrus king of Persia, so that he made a proclamation throughout all his kingdom, and also *put it* in writing, saying,

²Thus says Cyrus king of Persia: All the kingdoms of the earth the LORD God of heaven has given me. And He has

has appointed me to build a Temple for him at Jerusalem in Judah. ³May God be with all of you who are his people. You are free to go to Jerusalem in Judah and build the Temple of the Lord, the God of Israel, who is in Jerusalem. ⁴Those who stay behind, wherever they live, should support those who want to go. Give them silver and gold, supplies and cattle, and special gifts for the Temple of God in Jerusalem.

⁵Then the family leaders of Judah and Benjamin and the priests and Levites got ready to go to Jerusalem—everyone God had caused to want to go to Jerusalem to build the Temple of the Lord. ⁶All their neighbors helped them, giving them things made of silver and gold, along with supplies, cattle, valuable gifts, and special gifts for the Temple. ⁷Also, King Cyrus brought out the bowls and pans that belonged in the Temple of the Lord, which Nebuchadnezzar had taken from Jerusalem and put in the temple of his own god. ⁸Cyrus king of Persia had Mithredath the treasurer bring them and count them out for Sheshbazzar, the prince of Judah.

⁹He listed thirty gold dishes, one thousand silver dishes, twenty-nine pans, ¹⁰thirty gold bowls, four hundred ten matching silver bowls, and one thousand other pieces.

¹¹There was a total of fifty-four hundred pieces of gold and silver. Sheshbazzar brought all these things along when the captives went from Babylon to Jerusalem.

commanded me to build Him a house at Jerusalem which is in Judah. ³Who is among you of all His people? May his God be with him, and let him go up to Jerusalem which is in Judah, and build the house of the Lord God of Israel (He is God), which is in Jerusalem. ⁴And whoever is left in any place where he dwells, let the men of his place help him with silver and gold, with goods and livestock, besides the freewill offerings for the house of God which is in Jerusalem.

⁵Then the heads of the fathers' houses of Judah and Benjamin, and the priests and the Levites, with all whose spirits God had moved, arose to go up and build the house of the Lord which is in Jerusalem. ⁶And all those who were around them encouraged them with articles of silver and gold, with goods and livestock, and with precious things, besides all that was willingly offered.

⁷King Cyrus also brought out the articles of the house of the Lord, which Nebuchadnezzar had taken from Jerusalem and put in the temple of his gods; ⁸and Cyrus king of Persia brought them out by the hand of Mithredath the treasurer, and counted them out to Sheshbazzar the prince of Judah. ⁹This is the number of them: thirty gold platters, one thousand silver platters, twenty-nine knives, ¹⁰thirty gold basins, four hundred and ten silver basins of a similar kind, and one thousand other articles. ¹¹All the articles of gold and silver were five thousand four hundred. All these Sheshbazzar took with the captives who were brought from Babylon to Jerusalem.

DISCOVERY

Explore the Bible reading by discussing these questions.

2. What do you think it means when the Scripture says that God prompted the decree of the king to rebuild the temple?

_____

_____

_____

3. Why are the actions of King Cyrus significant in light of the plight of the Jews?

_____

_____

_____

4. What instructions did Cyrus give to the Jewish people?

_____

_____

_____

5. How did God cause some to want to go and not others?

_____

_____

_____

6. Why was it important for the people who stayed behind to support those who were willing to go to work on the Temple?

_____

_____

_____

INSPIRATION

Here is an uplifting thought from *The Inspirational Bible*.

Perhaps changes are in the air right now. Maybe you're in the midst of a decision. It's disrupting, isn't it? You like your branch. You've grown accustomed to it and it to you. And, like Joseph, you've been a pretty good branch-sitter. And then you hear the call. "I need you to go out on the limb and

. . . take a stand. Some of the local churches are organizing an anti-pornography campaign. They need some volunteers."

. . . move. Take your family and move overseas, I have a special work for you."

. . . forgive. It doesn't matter who hurt who first. What matters is that you go and build the bridge."

. . . evangelize. That new family down the block? They don't know anyone in town. Go meet them."

. . . sacrifice. The orphanage has a mortgage payment due this month. They can't meet it. Remember the bonus you received last week?"

Regardless of the nature of the call, the consequences are the same: civil war. Though your heart may say yes, your feet say no. Excuses blow numerously as golden leaves in an autumn wind. "That's not my talent." "It's time for someone else to take charge." "Not now. I'll get to it tomorrow."

But eventually you're left staring at a bare tree and a hard choice: His will or yours?

(From *God Came Near*
by Max Lucado)

RESPONSE

Use these questions to share more deeply with each other.

7. What can we learn from the example of the Israelites who obeyed God's call to rebuild the Temple?

_____

_____

_____

8. What fears or obstacles did these people face?

_____

_____

_____

9. Why do we sometimes hesitate to obey God's call?

_____

_____

_____

PRAYER

Father, we want to be people who are willing to give up everything to follow you. Help us to see that the most valuable things this world has to offer are worthless compared to the blessings you have in store for those who obey you. Open our ears to hear your call and help us to obey, whatever the cost.

JOURNALING

Take a few moments to record your personal insights from this lesson.

What step of obedience does God want me to take this week?

ADDITIONAL QUESTIONS

10. How does God communicate his will to us?

_____

_____

_____

11. Think of a time when you have found it difficult to obey God's call. What made it difficult?

_____

_____

_____

12. In what ways has God helped you accomplish the things he has asked you to do?

_____

_____

_____

For more Bible passages on obedience, see Leviticus 19:2; Acts 5:29; Romans 6; 2 Corinthians 7:1; Titus 3:1; Hebrews 12:13–14; 1 Peter 1:14; 1 John 3:24; 2 John 6.

To complete the Books of Ezra and Nehemiah during this twelve-part study, read Ezra 1:1–2:70.

ADDITIONAL THOUGHTS

LESSON TWO

DEMONSTRATING FAITH

REFLECTION

Begin your study by sharing thoughts on this question.

1. Think of a time when you felt especially vulnerable or weak. To whom did you turn for help?

_____

_____

_____

BIBLE READING

Read Ezra 3:1–11 from the NCV or the NKJV.

NCV

¹In the seventh month, after the Israelites were settled in their hometowns, they met together in Jerusalem. ²Then Jeshua son of Jozadak and his fellow priests joined Zerubbabel son of Shealtiel and began to build the altar of the God of Israel where they could offer burnt offerings, just as it is written in the Teachings of Moses, the man of God. ³Even though they were afraid of the people living around them, they built the altar where it had been before.

NKJV

¹And when the seventh month had come, and the children of Israel *were* in the cities, the people gathered together as one man to Jerusalem. ²Then Jeshua the son of Jozadak and his brethren the priests, and Zerubbabel the son of Shealtiel and his brethren, arose and built the altar of the God of Israel, to offer burnt offerings on it, as *it is* written in the Law of Moses the man of God. ³Though fear *had come* upon them because of the people of those

NCV

And they offered burnt offerings on it to the LORD morning and evening. ⁴Then, to obey what was written, they celebrated the Feast of Shelters. They offered the right number of sacrifices for each day of the festival. ⁵After the Feast of Shelters, they had regular sacrifices every day, as well as sacrifices for the New Moon and all the festivals commanded by the LORD. Also there were special offerings brought as gifts to the LORD. ⁶On the first day of the seventh month they began to bring burnt offerings to the LORD, but the foundation of the LORD's Temple had not yet been laid.

⁷Then they gave money to the bricklayers and carpenters. They also gave food, wine, and oil to the cities of Sidon and Tyre so they would float cedar logs from Lebanon to the seacoast town of Joppa. Cyrus king of Persia had given permission for this.

⁸In the second month of the second year after their arrival at the Temple of God in Jerusalem, Zerubbabel son of Shealtiel, Jeshua son of Jozadak, their fellow priests and Levites, and all who had returned from captivity to Jerusalem began to work. They chose Levites twenty years old and older to be in charge of the building of the Temple of the LORD. ⁹These men were in charge of the work of building the Temple of God: Jeshua and his sons and brothers; Kadmiel and his sons who were the descendants of Hodaviah; and the sons of Henadad and their sons and brothers. They were all Levites.

¹⁰The builders finished laying the foundation of the Temple of the LORD. Then the priests, dressed in their robes, stood with their trum-

NKJV

countries, they set the altar on its bases; and they offered burnt offerings on it to the LORD, *both* the morning and evening burnt offerings. ⁴They also kept the Feast of Tabernacles, as *it is* written, and *offered* the daily burnt offerings in the number required by ordinance for each day. ⁵Afterwards *they offered* the regular burnt offering, and *those* for New Moons and for all the appointed feasts of the LORD that were consecrated, and *those* of everyone who willingly offered a freewill offering to the LORD. ⁶From the first day of the seventh month they began to offer burnt offerings to the LORD, although the foundation of the temple of the LORD had not been laid. ⁷They also gave money to the masons and the carpenters, and food, drink, and oil to the people of Sidon and Tyre to bring cedar logs from Lebanon to the sea, to Joppa, according to the permission which they had from Cyrus king of Persia.

⁸Now in the second month of the second year of their coming to the house of God at Jerusalem, Zerubbabel the son of Shealtiel, Jeshua the son of Jozadak, and the rest of their brethren the priests and the Levites, and all those who had come out of the captivity to Jerusalem, began *work* and appointed the Levites from twenty years old and above to oversee the work of the house of the LORD. ⁹Then Jeshua *with* his sons and brothers, Kadmiel *with* his sons, and the sons of Judah, arose as one to oversee those working on the house of God: the sons of Henadad *with* their sons and their brethren the Levites.

¹⁰When the builders laid the foundation of the temple of the LORD, the priests stood in

NCV	NKJV

pets, and the Levites, the sons of Asaph, stood with their cymbals. They all took their places and praised the LORD just as David king of Israel had said to do. [11]With praise and thanksgiving, they sang to the LORD:

> "He is good;
>> his love for Israel continues forever."

And then all the people shouted loudly, "Praise the LORD! The foundation of his Temple has been laid."

their apparel with trumpets, and the Levites, the sons of Asaph, with cymbals, to praise the LORD, according to the ordinance of David king of Israel. [11]And they sang responsively, praising and giving thanks to the LORD:

> "For *He is* good,
>> For His mercy *endures* forever toward Israel."

Then all the people shouted with a great shout, when they praised the LORD, because the foundation of the house of the LORD was laid.

DISCOVERY

Explore the Bible reading by discussing these questions.

2. The Jews started building an altar almost immediately after they returned to their homeland. What does that say about their priorities?

_____

_____

_____

3. In light of their actions, what had the exiles learned during their years in captivity?

_____

_____

_____

4. What risks did the Jews take in building an altar and offering sacrifices to God?

_____

_____

_____

5. Why do you think it was important to the exiles to demonstrate publicly their faith in God?

_____

_____

_____

6. Why did the people celebrate the completion of the Temple's foundation?

_____

_____

_____

INSPIRATION

Here is an uplifting thought from *The Inspirational Bible*.

Faith is the belief that God is real and that God is good. Faith is not a mystical experience or a midnight vision or a voice in the forest. . . . It is a choice to believe that the one who made it all hasn't left it all and that he still sends light into the shadows and responds to gestures of faith. . . .

Faith is not the belief that God will do what you want. Faith is the belief that God will do what is right.

"Blessed are the dirt-poor, nothing-to-give, trapped-in-a-corner, destitute, diseased," Jesus said, "for theirs is the kingdom of heaven" (Matt. 5:3, my translation).

God's economy is upside down (or rightside up and ours is upside down!). God says that the more hopeless your circumstances, the more likely your salvation. The greater your cares, the more genuine your prayers. The darker the room, the greater the need for light. . . .

God's help is near and always available, but it is only given to those who seek it. Nothing results from apathy. . . .

Compared to God's part, our part is minuscule but necessary. We don't have to do much, but we do have to do something. Write a letter. Ask forgiveness. Call a counselor. Confess. Call Mom. Visit a doctor. Be baptized. Feed a hungry person. Pray. Teach. Go.

Do something that demonstrates faith. For faith with no effort is no faith at all. God will respond. He has never rejected a genuine gesture of faith. Never.

(From *He Still Moves Stones*
by Max Lucado)

RESPONSE

Use these questions to share more deeply with each other.

7. Why do we tend to forget God when times are good, only to turn to him when life becomes difficult?

_____

_____

_____

8. Explain how God has used a difficult experience in your life to strengthen your faith.

_____

_____

_____

9. In what ways does God honor the faith of his people?

_____

_____

_____

PRAYER

Father, we cherish your constant presence with us. You are always near and always ready to take us back when we have turned away from you. Forgive us, Father, for thinking that we don't need you. We ask that you would help us to be faithful, in good times and bad times. Give us the courage to tell the world that you are our God.

JOURNALING

Take a few moments to record your personal insights from this lesson.

What small step of faith am I willing to take today to demonstrate my trust in God?

ADDITIONAL QUESTIONS

10. In what circumstances is it tempting to remain silent about your faith?

_____

_____

_____

11. How can we overcome our fears about standing up for our beliefs?

_____

_____

_____

12. List some practical ways we can show others that we are Christians.

_____

_____

_____

For more Bible passages on faith, see Genesis 15:6; 2 Chronicles 20:20; Isaiah 7:9; Matthew 9:29; Acts 15:7–9; Romans 5:1; 10:17.

To complete the Books of Ezra and Nehemiah during this twelve-part study, read Ezra 3:1–4:24.

LESSON THREE

WORSHIP

REFLECTION

Begin your study by sharing thoughts on this question.

1. Think about what you enjoy most about the worship services at your church. Why?

_____

_____

_____

BIBLE READING

Read Ezra 6:13–22 from the NCV or the NKJV.

NCV

¹³So, Tattenai, the governor of Trans-Euphrates, Shethar-Bozenai, and their fellow workers carried out King Darius' order quickly and carefully. ¹⁴The older Jewish leaders continued to build and were successful because of the preaching of Haggai the prophet and Zechariah, a descendant of Iddo. They finished building the Temple as the God of Israel had commanded and as kings Cyrus, Darius, and Artaxerxes of Persia had ordered. ¹⁵The Temple was finished on the third day of the month of Adar in the sixth year Darius was king.

NKJV

¹³Then Tattenai, governor of *the region* beyond the River, Shethar-Boznai, and their companions diligently did according to what King Darius had sent. ¹⁴So the elders of the Jews built, and they prospered through the prophesying of Haggai the prophet and Zechariah the son of Iddo. And they built and finished *it*, according to the commandment of the God of Israel, and according to the command of Cyrus, Darius, and Artaxerxes king of Persia. ¹⁵Now the temple was finished on the third day of the month of Adar, which was in the sixth year of

NCV

[16]Then the people of Israel celebrated and gave the Temple to God to honor him. Everybody was happy: the priests, the Levites, and the rest of the Jewish people who had returned from captivity. [17]They gave the Temple to God by offering a hundred bulls, two hundred male sheep, and four hundred lambs as sacrifices. And as an offering to forgive the sins of all Israel, they offered twelve male goats, one goat for each tribe in Israel. [18]Then they put the priests and the Levites into their separate groups. Each group had a certain time to serve God in the Temple at Jerusalem as it is written in the Book of Moses.

[19]The Jewish people who returned from captivity celebrated the Passover on the fourteenth day of the first month. [20]The priests and Levites had made themselves clean. Then the Levites killed the Passover lambs for all the people who had returned from captivity, for their relatives the priests, and for themselves. [21]So all the people of Israel who returned from captivity ate the Passover lamb. So did the people who had given up the unclean ways of their non-Jewish neighbors in order to worship the LORD, the God of Israel. [22]For seven days they celebrated the Feast of Unleavened Bread in a very joyful way. The LORD had made them happy by changing the mind of the king of Assyria so that he helped them in the work on the Temple of the God of Israel.

NKJV

the reign of King Darius. [16]Then the children of Israel, the priests and the Levites and the rest of the descendants of the captivity, celebrated the dedication of this house of God with joy. [17]And they offered sacrifices at the dedication of this house of God, one hundred bulls, two hundred rams, four hundred lambs, and as a sin offering for all Israel twelve male goats, according to the number of the tribes of Israel. [18]They assigned the priests to their divisions and the Levites to their divisions, over the service of God in Jerusalem, as it is written in the Book of Moses.

[19]And the descendants of the captivity kept the Passover on the fourteenth *day* of the first month. [20]For the priests and the Levites had purified themselves; all of them *were ritually* clean. And they slaughtered the Passover *lambs* for all the descendants of the captivity, for their brethren the priests, and for themselves. [21]Then the children of Israel who had returned from the captivity ate together with all who had separated themselves from the filth of the nations of the land in order to seek the LORD God of Israel. [22]And they kept the Feast of Unleavened Bread seven days with joy; for the LORD made them joyful, and turned the heart of the king of Assyria toward them, to strengthen their hands in the work of the house of God, the God of Israel.

DISCOVERY

Explore the Bible reading by discussing these questions.

2. What factors contributed to the success of the Jewish leaders' building efforts?

_____

_____

_____

3. What was the focal point of the Israelites' celebration?

_____

_____

_____

4. Why did the people commemorate the completion of the Temple?

_____

_____

_____

5. What did some people give up in order to worship the God of Israel?

_____

_____

_____

6. What caused the Israelites to worship God with such joy?

_____

_____

_____

INSPIRATION

Here is an uplifting thought from *The Inspirational Bible*.

When you recognize God as Creator, you will admire him. When you recognize his wisdom, you will learn from him. When you discover his strength, you will rely on him. But only when he saves you will you worship him.

It's a "before and after" scenario. Before your rescue, you could easily keep God at a distance. Comfortably dismissed. Neatly shelved. Sure he was important, but so was your career. Your status. Your salary. He was high on your priority list, but he shared the spot with others.

Then came the storm . . . the rage . . . the fight . . . the ripped moorings . . . the starless night. Despair fell like a fog; your bearings were gone. In your heart, you knew there was no exit.

Turn to your career for help? Only if you want to hide from the storm . . . not escape it. Lean on your status for strength? A storm isn't impressed with your title. Rely on your salary for rescue? Many try . . . many fail.

Suddenly you are left with one option: God.

And when you ask . . . genuinely ask . . . he will come.

And from that moment on, he is not just a deity to admire, a teacher to observe, or a master to obey. He is the Savior. The Savior to be worshiped.

. . . A season of suffering is a small price to pay for a clear view of God.

(From *In the Eye of the Storm* by Max Lucado)

RESPONSE

Use these questions to share more deeply with each other.

7. What principles can we glean from this passage about how we should worship?

_____

_____

_____

8. In what ways can trials and testing lead to more meaningful worship?

_____

_____

_____

9. What can interfere with our worship?

_____

_____

_____

PRAYER

Father, forgive us for our feeble attempts at worship. We ask you to come alongside us and teach us what it means to worship you. Give us a glimpse of the intensity of your love for us and the depth of your mercy. Deepen our understanding and appreciation for what you have done, so that we may give you the praise and adoration you deserve.

JOURNALING

Take a few moments to record your personal insights from this lesson.

What reasons do I have to celebrate and worship God?

ADDITIONAL QUESTIONS

10. When has God provided for you in a spectacular way?

_____

_____

_____

11. How did God's provision impact your worship?

_____

_____

_____

12. In what ways can you gain a better understanding of what God has done for you?

_____

_____

_____

For more Bible passages on worship, see 2 Kings 17:36–39; 1 Chronicles 16:28–29; Psalm 95:6–7; John 4:24; Romans 12:1.

To complete the Books of Ezra and Nehemiah during this twelve-part study, read Ezra 5:1—6:22.

ADDITIONAL THOUGHTS

LESSON FOUR

RELYING ON GOD

REFLECTION

Begin your study by sharing thoughts on this question.

1. How have you experienced God's protection or provision recently?

_____

_____

_____

BIBLE READING

Read Ezra 8:21–32 from the NCV or the NKJV.

NCV

²¹There by the Ahava Canal, I announced we would all give up eating and humble ourselves before our God. We would ask God for a safe trip for ourselves, our children, and all our possessions. ²²I was ashamed to ask the king for soldiers and horsemen to protect us from enemies on the road. We had said to the king, "Our God helps everyone who obeys him, but he is very angry with all who reject him."²³So we gave up eating and prayed to our God about our trip, and he answered our prayers.

NKJV

²¹Then I proclaimed a fast there at the river of Ahava, that we might humble ourselves before our God, to seek from Him the right way for us and our little ones and all our possessions. ²²For I was ashamed to request of the king an escort of soldiers and horsemen to help us against the enemy on the road, because we had spoken to the king, saying, "The hand of our God is upon all those for good who seek Him, but His power and His wrath are against all those who forsake Him."²³So we fasted and

NCV

²⁴Then I chose twelve of the priests who were leaders, Sherebiah, Hashabiah, and ten of their relatives. ²⁵I weighed the offering of silver and gold and the utensils given for the Temple of our God, and I gave them to the twelve priests I had chosen. The king, the people who advised him, his officers, and all the Israelites there with us had given these things for the Temple. ²⁶I weighed out and gave them about fifty thousand pounds of silver, about seventy-five hundred pounds of silver objects, and about seventy-five hundred pounds of gold. ²⁷I gave them twenty gold bowls that weighed about nineteen pounds and two fine pieces of polished bronze that were as valuable as gold.

²⁸Then I said to the priests, "You and these utensils belong to the LORD for his service. The silver and gold are gifts to the LORD, the God of your ancestors. ²⁹Guard these things carefully. In Jerusalem, weigh them in front of the leading priests, Levites, and the leaders of the family groups of Israel in the rooms of the Temple of the LORD." ³⁰So the priests and Levites accepted the silver, the gold, and the utensils that had been weighed to take them to the Temple of our God in Jerusalem.

³¹On the twelfth day of the first month we left the Ahava Canal and started toward Jerusalem. Our God helped us and protected us from enemies and robbers along the way. ³²Finally we arrived in Jerusalem where we rested three days.

NKJV

entreated our God for this, and He answered our prayer.

²⁴And I separated twelve of the leaders of the priests—Sherebiah, Hashabiah, and ten of their brethren with them—²⁵and weighed out to them the silver, the gold, and the articles, the offering for the house of our God which the king and his counselors and his princes, and all Israel *who were* present, had offered. ²⁶I weighed into their hand six hundred and fifty talents of silver, silver articles *weighing* one hundred talents, one hundred talents of gold, ²⁷twenty gold basins *worth* a thousand drachmas, and two vessels of fine polished bronze, precious as gold. ²⁸And I said to them, "You *are* holy to the LORD; the articles *are* holy also; and the silver and the gold *are* a freewill offering to the LORD God of your fathers. ²⁹Watch and keep *them* until you weigh *them* before the leaders of the priests and the Levites and heads of the fathers' *houses* of Israel in Jerusalem, *in* the chambers of the house of the LORD." ³⁰So the priests and the Levites received the silver and the gold and the articles by weight, to bring *them* to Jerusalem to the house of our God.

³¹Then we departed from the river of Ahava on the twelfth *day* of the first month, to go to Jerusalem. And the hand of our God was upon us, and He delivered us from the hand of the enemy and from ambush along the road. ³²So we came to Jerusalem, and stayed there three days.

DISCOVERY

Explore the Bible reading by discussing these questions.

2. How did the Israelites humble themselves before God by fasting? How does giving up food encourage humility?

_____

_____

_____

3. Why was humbling themselves before they prayed a good idea?

_____

_____

_____

4. Why was Ezra unwilling to ask the king for help?

_____

_____

_____

5. Why were the people so concerned about the safety of their possessions on this journey?

_____

_____

_____

6. In what ways did God answer the prayers of the Israelites?

_____

_____

_____

INSPIRATION

Here is an uplifting thought from *The Inspirational Bible*.

To recognize God as Lord is to acknowledge that he is sovereign and supreme in the universe. To accept him as Savior is to accept his gift of salvation offered on the cross. To regard him as a Father is to go a step further. Ideally, a father is the one in your life who provides and protects. That is exactly what God has done.

He has provided for your needs. He has protected you from harm. He has adopted you. And he has given you his name.

God has proven himself as a faithful father. Now it falls to us to be trusting children. Let God give you what your family doesn't. Let him fill the void others have left. Rely upon him for your affirmation and encouragement. Look at Paul's words: "You are God's child and *God will give you the blessing promised*, because you are his child" (Gal. 4:7, emphasis added).

(From *He Still Moves Stones* by Max Lucado)

RESPONSE

Use these questions to share more deeply with each other.

7. What message do we send to others when we trust God to help us, instead of relying on our own strength?

_____

_____

_____

8. In what ways can our desire for control interfere with our dependence on God?

_____

_____

_____

9. What inhibits our ability to trust God with our needs?

_____

_____

_____

PRAYER

Father, thank you for your constant care for us. You have proven time and time again that you are a loving father who always protects and provides for his children. Help us to put our full confidence in you, and teach us to trust you with our daily needs and future concerns. May we rest secure in your loving arms.

JOURNALING

Take a few moments to record your personal insights from this lesson.

In what area of my life do I need to trust God more?

ADDITIONAL QUESTIONS

10. In what circumstances do you tend to take matters into your own hands, rather than trust God?

_____

_____

_____

11. In what ways has God proven himself as a faithful father to you?

_____

_____

_____

12. How does remembering God's care for you in the past change your attitude toward your present needs?

_____

_____

_____

For more Bible passages on trusting God, see Psalm 62:8; 143:8; Proverbs 29:25; Isaiah 25:9; Nahum 1:7; Romans 10:11.

To complete the Books of Ezra and Nehemiah during this twelve-part study, read Ezra 7:1—8:36.

ADDITIONAL THOUGHTS

LESSON FIVE

DEALING WITH GUILT

REFLECTION

Begin your study by sharing thoughts on this question.

1. Think of a time when you experienced relief from a burden of guilt. Describe how this felt.

_____

_____

_____

BIBLE READING

Read Ezra 9:1–15 from the NCV or the NKJV.

NCV

¹After these things had been done, the leaders came to me and said, "Ezra, the Israelites, including the priests and Levites, have not kept themselves separate from the people around us. Those neighbors do evil things, as the Canaanites, Hittites, Perizzites, Jebusites, Ammonites, Moabites, Egyptians, and Amorites did. ²The Israelite men and their sons have married these women. They have mixed the people who belong to God with the people around them. The leaders and officers of

NKJV

¹When these things were done, the leaders came to me, saying, "The people of Israel and the priests and the Levites have not separated themselves from the peoples of the lands, with respect to the abominations of the Canaanites, the Hittites, the Perizzites, the Jebusites, the Ammonites, the Moabites, the Egyptians, and the Amorites. ²"For they have taken some of their daughters _as wives_ for themselves and their sons, so that the holy seed is mixed with the peoples of _those_ lands. Indeed, the hand of

Israel have led the rest of the Israelites to do this unfaithful thing."

³When I heard this, I angrily tore my robe and coat, pulled hair from my head and beard, and sat down in shock. ⁴Everyone who trembled in fear at the word of the God of Israel gathered around me because of the unfaithfulness of the captives who had returned. I sat there in shock until the evening sacrifice.

⁵At the evening sacrifice I got up from where I had shown my shame. My robe and coat were torn, and I fell on my knees with my hands spread out to the LORD my God. ⁶I prayed,

"My God, I am too ashamed and embarrassed to lift up my face to you, my God, because our sins are so many. They are higher than our heads. Our guilt even reaches up to the sky. ⁷From the days of our ancestors until now, our guilt has been great. Because of our sins, we, our kings, and our priests have been punished by the sword and captivity. Foreign kings have taken away our things and shamed us, even as it is today.

⁸"But now, for a short time, the LORD our God has been kind to us. He has let some of us come back from captivity and has let us live in safety in his holy place. And so our God gives us hope and a little relief from our slavery. ⁹Even though we are slaves, our God has not left us. He caused the kings of Persia to be kind to us and has given us new life. We can rebuild the Temple and repair its ruins. And he has given us a wall to protect us in Judah and Jerusalem.

¹⁰"But now, our God, what can we say after you have done all this? We have disobeyed your commands ¹¹that you gave through your

the leaders and rulers has been foremost in this trespass."³So when I heard this thing, I tore my garment and my robe, and plucked out some of the hair of my head and beard, and sat down astonished. ⁴Then everyone who trembled at the words of the God of Israel assembled to me, because of the transgression of those who had been carried away captive, and I sat astonished until the evening sacrifice.

⁵At the evening sacrifice I arose from my fasting; and having torn my garment and my robe, I fell on my knees and spread out my hands to the LORD my God. ⁶And I said: "O my God, I am too ashamed and humiliated to lift up my face to You, my God; for our iniquities have risen higher than *our* heads, and our guilt has grown up to the heavens. ⁷Since the days of our fathers to this day we *have been* very guilty, and for our iniquities we, our kings, *and* our priests have been delivered into the hand of the kings of the lands, to the sword, to captivity, to plunder, and to humiliation, as *it is* this day. ⁸And now for a little while grace has been *shown* from the LORD our God, to leave us a remnant to escape, and to give us a peg in His holy place, that our God may enlighten our eyes and give us a measure of revival in our bondage.

⁹"For we *were* slaves. Yet our God did not forsake us in our bondage; but He extended mercy to us in the sight of the kings of Persia, to revive us, to repair the house of our God, to rebuild its ruins, and to give us a wall in Judah and Jerusalem. ¹⁰And now, O our God, what shall we say after this? For we have forsaken Your commandments, ¹¹which You command-

NCV

servants the prophets. You said, 'The land you are entering to own is ruined; the people living there have spoiled it by the evil they do. Their evil filled the land with uncleanness from one end to the other. [12]So do not let your daughters marry their sons, and do not let their daughters marry your sons. Do not wish for their peace or success. Then you will be strong and eat the good things of the land. Then you can leave this land to your descendants forever.'

[13]"What has happened to us is our own fault. We have done evil things, and our guilt is great. But you, our God, have punished us less than we deserve; you have left a few of us alive. [14]We should not again break your commands by allowing marriages with these wicked people. If we did, you would get angry enough to destroy us, and none of us would be left alive. [15]LORD, God of Israel, by your goodness a few of us are left alive today. We admit that we are guilty and none of us should be allowed to stand before you."

NKJV

ed by Your servants the prophets, saying, 'The land which you are entering to possess is an unclean land, with the uncleanness of the peoples of the lands, with their abominations which have filled it from one end to another with their impurity. [12]Now therefore, do not give your daughters as wives for their sons, nor take their daughters to your sons; and never seek their peace or prosperity, that you may be strong and eat the good of the land, and leave *it* as an inheritance to your children forever.' [13]And after all that has come upon us for our evil deeds and for our great guilt, since You our God have punished us less than our iniquities *deserve,* and have given us *such* deliverance as this, [14]should we again break Your commandments, and join in marriage with the people *committing* these abominations? Would You not be angry with us until You had consumed *us,* so that *there would be* no remnant or survivor? [15]O LORD God of Israel, You *are* righteous, for we are left as a remnant, as *it is* this day. Here we *are* before You, in our guilt, though no one can stand before You because of this!"

DISCOVERY

Explore the Bible reading by discussing these questions.

2. Why did the Jewish leaders bring their problem to Ezra's attention?

_____

_____

_____

3. How did Ezra react to the sins of his people?

_____

_____

_____

4. Who shared in Ezra's remorse for the people's unfaithfulness to God?

_____

_____

_____

5. Why did Ezra include himself in his prayer of repentance, even though he had remained faithful to God?

_____

_____

_____

6. Why was it difficult for the Israelites to remember God's mercy and justice?

_____

_____

_____

INSPIRATION

Here is an uplifting thought from *The Inspirational Bible*.

You lose your temper. You lust. You fall. You take a drag. You buy a drink. You kiss the woman. You follow the crowd. You rationalize. You say yes. You sign your name. You forget who you are. You walk into her room. You look in the window. You break your promise. You buy the magazine. You lie. You covet. You stomp your feet and demand your way. You deny your Master.

It's David disrobing Bathsheba. It's Adam accepting the fruit from Eve. It's Abraham lying about Sarah. It's Peter denying that he ever knew Jesus. It's Noah, drunk and naked in his tent. It's Lot in bed with his own daughter. It's your worst nightmare. It's sudden. It's sin.

Satan numbs our awareness and short-circuits our self-control. We know what we are doing and yet can't believe that we are doing it. In the fog of weakness we want to stop but haven't the will to do so. We want to turn around, but our feet won't move. We want to run and, pitifully, we want to stay....

Confusion. Guilt. Rationalization. Despair. It all hits. It hits hard. We numbly pick ourselves up and stagger back into our world. "Oh God, what have I done?" "Should I tell someone?" "I'll never do it again." "My God, can you forgive me?"

No one who is reading these words is free from the treachery of sudden sin. No one is immune to this trick of perdition. This demon of hell can scale the highest monastery wall, penetrate the deepest faith, and desecrate the purest home.

Some of you know exactly what I mean. You could write these words better than I, couldn't you? Some of you, like me, have tumbled so often that the stench of Satan's breath is far from a novelty. You've asked for God's forgiveness so often that you worry that the well of mercy might run dry....

Romans chapter 7 is the Emancipation Proclamation for those of us who have a tendency to tumble. Look at verse 15: "I do not understand what I do. For what I want to do I do not do, but what I hate I do."

Sound familiar? Read on. Verses 18–19: "For I have the desire to do what is good, but I cannot carry it out. For what I do is not the good I want to do; no, the evil I do not want to do—this I keep on doing."

Man, that fellow has been reading my diary!

"What a wretched man I am! Who will rescue me from the body of death?" (v. 24).

Please, Paul, don't stop there! Is there no oasis in this barrenness of guilt? There is. Thank God and drink deeply as you read verse 25 and verse 1 of chapter 8: "Thanks be to God—through Jesus Christ our Lord! . . . Therefore there is now no condemnation for those who are in Christ Jesus."

Amen. There it is. You read it right. Underline it if you wish. For those *in* Christ there is *no* condemnation. Absolutely none. Claim the promise. Memorize the words. Accept the cleansing. Throw out the guilt. Praise the Lord.

(From *On the Anvil* by Max Lucado)

RESPONSE

Use these questions to share more deeply with each other.

7. What are some typical ways we deal with a guilty conscience?

_____

_____

_____

8. List new insights from this passage about the right way to handle guilt.

_____

_____

_____

9. Why is it tempting to ignore a guilty conscience?

_____

_____

_____

PRAYER

We pray, Father, that you would help us to be sensitive to the conviction of your Spirit. Help us to repent of sin quickly, never letting it take root in our lives. And teach us to release our guilt to you and to forgive ourselves, so that we may not live in bondage to our failures. May we always be thankful for your mercy and grace.

JOURNALING

Take a few moments to record your personal insights from this lesson.

How do I need to change the way I deal with guilt?

ADDITIONAL QUESTIONS

10. Sometimes guilt is productive and sometimes it is harmful. What is the difference between the two?

_____

_____

_____

11. Why do some people hold on to their guilt after they have confessed their sin to God?

_____

_____

_____

12. In what area of your life do you need to accept God's forgiveness?

_____

_____

_____

For more Bible passages on guilt, see Psalm 32:1–5; 38:1–4; Isaiah 6:5–7; Jeremiah 2:22–35; Hebrews 10:2–22.

To complete the Books of Ezra and Nehemiah during this twelve-part study, read Ezra 9:1–15.

LESSON SIX

TRUE REPENTANCE

REFLECTION

Begin your study by sharing thoughts on this question.

1. Think of a time when you asked a friend to forgive you. How did it feel to receive forgiveness?

_____

_____

_____

BIBLE READING

Read Ezra 10:1–17 from the NCV or the NKJV.

NCV

¹As Ezra was praying and confessing and crying and throwing himself down in front of the Temple, a large group of Israelite men, women, and children gathered around him who were also crying loudly. ²Then Shecaniah son of Jehiel the Elamite said to Ezra, "We have been unfaithful to our God by marrying women from the peoples around us. But even so, there is still hope for Israel. ³Now let us make an agreement before our God. We will send away all these women and their children as you

NKJV

¹Now while Ezra was praying, and while he was confessing, weeping, and bowing down before the house of God, a very large assembly of men, women, and children gathered to him from Israel; for the people wept very bitterly. ²And Shechaniah the son of Jehiel, *one* of the sons of Elam, spoke up and said to Ezra, "We have trespassed against our God, and have taken pagan wives from the peoples of the land; yet now there is hope in Israel in spite of this. ³Now therefore, let us make a covenant with our

and those who respect the commands of our God advise. Let it be done to obey God's Teachings. ⁴Get up, Ezra. You are in charge, and we will support you. Have courage and do it."

⁵So Ezra got up and made the priests, Levites, and all the people of Israel promise to do what was suggested; and they promised. ⁶Then Ezra left the Temple and went to the room of Jehohanan son of Eliashib. While Ezra was there, he did not eat or drink, because he was still sad about the unfaithfulness of the captives who had returned.

⁷They sent an order in Judah and Jerusalem for all the captives who had returned to meet together in Jerusalem. ⁸Whoever did not come to Jerusalem within three days would lose his property and would no longer be a member of the community of the returned captives. That was the decision of the officers and older leaders.

⁹So within three days all the people of Judah and Benjamin gathered in Jerusalem. It was the twentieth day of the ninth month. All the people were sitting in the open place in front of the Temple and were upset because of the meeting and because it was raining. ¹⁰Ezra the priest stood up and said to them, "You have been unfaithful and have married non-Jewish women. You have made Israel more guilty. ¹¹Now, confess it to the LORD, the God of your ancestors. Do his will and separate yourselves from the people living around you and from your non-Jewish wives."

¹²Then the whole group answered Ezra with a loud voice, "Ezra, you're right! We must do what you say. ¹³But there are many people here,

God to put away all these wives and those who have been born to them, according to the advice of my master and of those who tremble at the commandment of our God; and let it be done according to the law. ⁴Arise, for *this* matter *is* your *responsibility*. We also *are* with you. Be of good courage, and do *it*."

⁵Then Ezra arose, and made the leaders of the priests, the Levites, and all Israel swear an oath that they would do according to this word. So they swore an oath. ⁶Then Ezra rose up from before the house of God, and went into the chamber of Jehohanan the son of Eliashib; and *when* he came there, he ate no bread and drank no water, for he mourned because of the guilt of those from the captivity.

⁷And they issued a proclamation throughout Judah and Jerusalem to all the descendants of the captivity, that they must gather at Jerusalem, ⁸and that whoever would not come within three days, according to the instructions of the leaders and elders, all his property would be confiscated, and he himself would be separated from the assembly of those from the captivity.

⁹So all the men of Judah and Benjamin gathered at Jerusalem within three days. It *was* the ninth month, on the twentieth of the month; and all the people sat in the open square of the house of God, trembling because of *this* matter and because of heavy rain. ¹⁰Then Ezra the priest stood up and said to them, "You have transgressed and have taken pagan wives, adding to the guilt of Israel. ¹¹Now therefore, make confession to the LORD God of your fathers, and do His will; separate yourselves

NCV

and it's the rainy season. We can't stand outside, and this problem can't be solved in a day or two, because we have sinned badly. [14]Let our officers make a decision for the whole group. Then let everyone in our towns who has married a non-Jewish woman meet with the older leaders and judges of each town at a planned time, until the hot anger of our God turns away from us." [15]Only Jonathan son of Asahel, Jahzeiah son of Tikvah, Meshullam, and Shabbethai the Levite were against the plan.

[16]So the returned captives did what was suggested. Ezra the priest chose men who were leaders of the family groups and named one from each family division. On the first day of the tenth month they sat down to study each case. [17]By the first day of the first month, they had finished with all the men who had married non-Jewish women.

NKJV

from the peoples of the land, and from the pagan wives."

[12]Then all the assembly answered and said with a loud voice, "Yes! As you have said, so we must do. [13]But *there are* many people; *it is* the season for heavy rain, and we are not able to stand outside. Nor *is this* the work of one or two days, for *there are* many of us who have transgressed in this matter. [14]Please, let the leaders of our entire assembly stand; and let all those in our cities who have taken pagan wives come at appointed times, together with the elders and judges of their cities, until the fierce wrath of our God is turned away from us in this matter." [15]Only Jonathan the son of Asahel and Jahaziah the son of Tikvah opposed this, and Meshullam and Shabbethai the Levite gave them support.

[16]Then the descendants of the captivity did so. And Ezra the priest, *with* certain heads of the fathers' *households,* were set apart by the fathers' *households,* each of them by name; and they sat down on the first day of the tenth month to examine the matter. [17]By the first day of the first month they finished *questioning* all the men who had taken pagan wives.

DISCOVERY

Explore the Bible reading by discussing these questions.

2. What do you think prompted the Jewish exiles to acknowledge and confess their sin?

_____

_____

_____

3. What was Ezra's attitude toward the unfaithfulness of his people?

_____

_____

_____

4. In what ways did the people prove that they were truly sorry for their sins?

_____

_____

_____

5. What steps did the Israelites take to restore their relationship with God?

_____

_____

_____

6. Why was it important for the exiles to separate themselves from their non-Jewish wives?

_____

_____

_____

INSPIRATION

Here is an uplifting thought from *The Inspirational Bible*.

"If we confess our sins . . ." The biggest word in Scriptures just might be that two letter one, if. For confessing sins—admitting failure—is exactly what prisoners of pride refuse to do.

"Well, I may not be perfect, but I'm better than Hitler and certainly kinder than Idi Amin!"

"Me a sinner? Oh, sure, I get rowdy every so often, but I'm a pretty good ol' boy."

"Listen, I'm just as good as the next guy. I pay my taxes. I coach the Little League team. I even make donations to Red Cross. Why, God's probably proud to have someone like me on his team."

Justification. Rationalization. Comparison. These are the tools of the jailbird. They sound good. They sound familiar. They even sound American. But in the kingdom, they sound hollow. . . .

When you get to the point of sorrow for your sins, when you admit that you have no other option but to cast all your cares on him, and when there is truly no other one that you can call, then cast all your cares on him, for he is waiting.

(From *The Applause of Heaven*
by Max Lucado)

RESPONSE

Use these questions to share more deeply with each other.

7. Why do we tend to downplay the importance of repentance?

_____

_____

_____

8. How would you define true repentance?

_____

_____

_____

9. Explain why confession is not enough by itself.

_____

_____

_____

PRAYER

Father, we are unworthy to stand in your presence, yet through the blood of your Son, Jesus Christ, we come to you for mercy. Remind us often, Father, of the importance of repentance. Give us strength through your Holy Spirit to turn away from our sin. And Father, show us how to deepen our relationship with you.

JOURNALING

Take a few moments to record your personal insights from this lesson.

Is there any area of my life in which I need to repent?

ADDITIONAL QUESTIONS

10. In what ways can unconfessed sin affect our relationship with God and others?

_____

_____

_____

11. In what ways do we treat God's mercy lightly?

_____

_____

_____

12. How can we express our thanks to God for his forgiveness?

_____

_____

_____

For more Bible passages on repentance, see Jeremiah 15:19; Ezekiel 18:30–32; Acts 3:19; Romans 2:4; 2 Corinthians 7:9–10; 2 Peter 3:9.

To complete the Books of Ezra and Nehemiah during this twelve-part study, read Ezra 10:1–44.

NEHEMIAH

INTRODUCTION

You are about to meet the Abraham Lincoln of the Old Testament. A respected leader with a tender heart. You will see his tears in the Oval Office as he weeps for people oppressed and vulnerable.

You are about to meet the General George Patton of the Old Testament. A rugged leader. Intolerant of compromise. Relentless in demanding perfection. He punished those who were soft by pushing them down and cursing their names.

You are about to meet the Winston Churchill of the Old Testament. A statesman. Tested and tried. Resisting the enemies who seek to lure him away from the task. Rising above the squabbling factions who could distract him.

The tenderness of Lincoln. The fire of Patton. The savvy of Churchill. All found in the same man.

Nehemiah.

When we meet him he is wearing the robe of royalty. He is the king's cupbearer. But though he was in a position of power, his heart beat for the people in Israel. He was a Hebrew in Persia. When word reached him that the Temple was being reconstructed, he grew anxious. He knew there was no wall to protect it.

Nehemiah invited God to use him to save the city. God answered his prayer by softening the heart of the Persian king. Artaxerxes gave not only his blessing, but also supplies to be used in the project.

Nehemiah exchanged the royal robe for coveralls and got to work. The project took twelve years and was uphill all the way. He was accused of everything from allowing faulty construction to being power-hungry. In spite of grumpy workers and lurking enemies, he made it. With the wall built and the enemy silent, the people rejoiced and Nehemiah went back to Persia.

After twelve years he returned. The walls were strong, but the people had gone to pot. Faith was forgotten and discipline was a bad word. So Nehemiah got busy again. He went to his closet, hung up his royal robe, bypassed his coveralls, dusted off his frock, and set about the task of teaching the people a few things about morality. He didn't mince words. "I argued with those people, put curses on them, hit some of them, and pulled out their hair" (13:25). Not what you'd call a typical Bible class.

But Nehemiah wasn't what you'd call a typical fellow.

LESSON SEVEN

PRAYER

REFLECTION

Begin your study by sharing thoughts on this question.

1. Think of a person whom you consider to be a prayer warrior. How has that person's life been an example to you?

_____

_____

_____

BIBLE READING

Read Nehemiah 1:1–10 from the NCV or the NKJV.

NCV

¹These are the words of Nehemiah son of Hacaliah.

In the month of Kislev in the twentieth year, I, Nehemiah, was in the capital city of Susa. ²One of my brothers named Hanani came with some other men from Judah. I asked them about Jerusalem and the Jewish people who lived through the captivity.

³They answered me, "Those who are left from the captivity are back in Judah, but they are in much trouble and are full of shame. The

NKJV

¹The words of Nehemiah the son of Hachaliah.

It came to pass in the month of Chislev, *in* the twentieth year, as I was in Shushan the citadel, ²that Hanani one of my brethren came with men from Judah; and I asked them concerning the Jews who had escaped, who had survived the captivity, and concerning Jerusalem. ³And they said to me, "The survivors who are left from the captivity in the province *are* there in great distress and reproach. The

NCV

wall around Jerusalem is broken down, and its gates have been burned."

⁴When I heard these things, I sat down and cried for several days. I was sad and ate nothing. I prayed to the God of heaven, ⁵"LORD, God of heaven, you are the great God who is to be respected. You are loyal, and you keep your agreement with those who love you and obey your commands. ⁶Look and listen carefully. Hear the prayer that I, your servant, am praying to you day and night for your servants, the Israelites. I confess the sins we Israelites have done against you. My father's family and I have sinned against you. ⁷We have been wicked toward you and have not obeyed the commands, rules, and laws you gave your servant Moses.

⁸"Remember what you taught your servant Moses, saying, 'If you are unfaithful, I will scatter you among the nations. ⁹But if you return to me and obey my commands, I will gather your people from the far ends of the earth. And I will bring them from captivity to where I have chosen to be worshiped.'

¹⁰"They are your servants and your people, whom you have saved with your great strength and power."

NKJV

wall of Jerusalem *is* also broken down, and its gates *are burned* with fire."

⁴So it was, when I heard these words, that I sat down and wept, and mourned *for many* days; I was fasting and praying before the God of heaven.

⁵And I said: "I pray, LORD God of heaven, O great and awesome God, *You* who keep *Your* covenant and mercy with those who love You and observe Your commandments, ⁶please let Your ear be attentive and Your eyes open, that You may hear the prayer of Your servant which I pray before You now, day and night, for the children of Israel Your servants, and confess the sins of the children of Israel which we have sinned against You. Both my father's house and I have sinned. ⁷We have acted very corruptly against You, and have not kept the commandments, the statutes, nor the ordinances which You commanded Your servant Moses. ⁸Remember, I pray, the word that You commanded Your servant Moses, saying, '*If* you are unfaithful, I will scatter you among the nations; ⁹but *if* you return to Me, and keep My commandments and do them, though some of you were cast out to the farthest part of the heavens, *yet* I will gather them from there, and bring them to the place which I have chosen as a dwelling for My name.' ¹⁰Now these *are* Your servants and Your people, whom You have redeemed by Your great power, and by Your strong hand.

DISCOVERY

Explore the Bible reading by discussing these questions.

2. In what ways did Nehemiah show his concern for the captives who had returned to Jerusalem?

_____

_____

_____

3. What was Nehemiah's first response when faced with a seemingly hopeless predicament?

_____

_____

_____

4. What does Nehemiah's prayer reveal about his view of himself and of God?

_____

_____

_____

5. How do you think prayer prepared Nehemiah to lead his people?

_____

_____

_____

6. Why would Nehemiah's position of authority be an asset in improving the situation?

_____

_____

_____

INSPIRATION

Here is an uplifting thought from *The Inspirational Bible*.

Nehemiah 1 is a blend of prayer and action. All who lead must place a high priority on prayer. Why is prayer so important? Here are the four shortest reasons I know.

Prayer *makes me wait*. I cannot pray and act at the same time. I have to wait to act until I finish praying. Prayer forces me to leave the situation with God; it makes me wait.

Secondly, prayer *clears my vision*. Southern California often has an overhanging weather problem in the mornings because of its coastal location until the sun "burns through" the morning fog. Prayer does that. When you first face a situation, is it foggy? Prayer will "burn through." Your vision will clear so you can see through God's eyes.

Thirdly, prayer *quiets my heart*. I cannot worry and pray at the same time. I am doing one or the other. Prayer makes me quiet. It replaces anxiety with a calm spirit. Knees don't knock when we kneel on them!

Fourthly, prayer *activates my faith*. After praying I am more prone to trust God. And how petty and negative and critical I am when I don't pray! Prayer sets faith on fire.

Don't just fill the margins in your Bible with words and thoughts about ways a leader prays. Do it! Don't just stop with just a sterile theology of prayer. Pray! Prayer was the first major step Nehemiah took in his journey to effective leadership....

... The Lord is the Specialist we need for those uncrossable and impossible experiences. He delights in accomplishing what we cannot pull off. But He awaits our cry. He listens for our request. Nehemiah was quick to call for help. His favorite position when faced with problems was the kneeling position.

(From *Hand Me Another Brick*
by Charles Swindoll)

RESPONSE

Use these questions to share more deeply with each other.

7. If God knows all of our fears, desires, and needs, why does he want us to pray about them?

_____

_____

_____

8. Based on this passage, list several ingredients of effective prayer.

_____

_____

_____

9. What ingredients of Nehemiah's prayer do you want to add to your prayer life?

_____

_____

_____

PRAYER

Father, we are prone to worry and to complain about our problems. We struggle to solve things on our own, instead of depending on you. Forgive us, Father, for living as though we don't need you. Teach us to turn to you first, to face every challenge in your strength, and to give you praise for what you accomplish through us.

JOURNALING

Take a few moments to record your personal insights from this lesson.

For what task or situation in my life do I need to ask for God's guidance and help?

ADDITIONAL QUESTIONS

10. In what ways can prayer change a person's attitude toward life's difficulties?

_____

_____

_____

11. Describe a time when prayer helped you through a difficult experience.

_____

_____

_____

12. In what ways does God bless those who continually turn to him in prayer?

_____

_____

_____

For more Bible passages on prayer, see 1 Samuel 7:7–9; Psalm 6:9; 32:6; Proverbs 15:8,29; Matthew 14:23; 21:22; 26:36; Ephesians 6:18; Philippians 4:6–7; Colossians 4:2; 1 Peter 3:12.

To complete the Books of Ezra and Nehemiah during this twelve-part study, read Nehemiah 1:1–11.

ADDITIONAL THOUGHTS

LESSON EIGHT

GOD'S PROTECTION

REFLECTION

Begin your study by sharing thoughts on this question.

1. Think of a time when God protected you from danger. How did that experience increase your faith?

_____

_____

_____

BIBLE READING

Read Nehemiah 2:1–20 from the NCV or the NKJV.

NCV

¹It was the month of Nisan in the twentieth year Artaxerxes was king. He wanted some wine, so I took some and gave it to the king. I had not been sad in his presence before. ²So the king said, "Why does your face look sad even though you are not sick? Your heart must be sad."

Then I was very afraid. ³I said to the king, "May the king live forever! My face is sad because the city where my ancestors are buried

NKJV

¹And it came to pass in the month of Nisan, in the twentieth year of King Artaxerxes, *when* wine *was* before him, that I took the wine and gave it to the king. Now I had never been sad in his presence before. ²Therefore the king said to me, "Why *is* your face sad, since you *are* not sick? This *is* nothing but sorrow of heart."

So I became dreadfully afraid, ³and said to the king, "May the king live forever! Why should my face not be sad, when the city, the place of

NCV

lies in ruins, and its gates have been destroyed by fire."

⁴Then the king said to me, "What do you want?"

First I prayed to the God of heaven. ⁵Then I answered the king, "If you are willing and if I have pleased you, send me to the city in Judah where my ancestors are buried so I can rebuild it."

⁶The queen was sitting next to the king. He asked me, "How long will your trip take, and when will you get back?" It pleased the king to send me, so I set a time.

⁷I also said to him, "If you are willing, give me letters for the governors of Trans-Euphrates. Tell them to let me pass safely through their lands on my way to Judah. ⁸And may I have a letter for Asaph, the keeper of the king's forest, telling him to give me timber? I will need it to make boards for the gates of the palace, which is by the Temple, and for the city wall, and for the house in which I will live." So the king gave me the letters, because God was showing kindness to me. ⁹Then I went to the governors of Trans-Euphrates and gave them the king's letters. The king had also sent army officers and soldiers on horses with me.

¹⁰When Sanballat the Horonite and Tobiah the Ammonite officer heard about this, they were upset that someone had come to help the Israelites.

¹¹I went to Jerusalem and stayed there three days. ¹²Then at night I started out with a few men. I had not told anyone what God had caused me to do for Jerusalem. There were no animals with me except the one I was riding.

NKJV

my fathers' tombs, *lies* waste, and its gates are burned with fire?"

⁴Then the king said to me, "What do you request?"

So I prayed to the God of heaven. ⁵And I said to the king, "If it pleases the king, and if your servant has found favor in your sight, I ask that you send me to Judah, to the city of my fathers' tombs, that I may rebuild it."

⁶Then the king said to me (the queen also sitting beside him), "How long will your journey be? And when will you return?" So it pleased the king to send me; and I set him a time.

⁷Furthermore I said to the king, "If it pleases the king, let letters be given to me for the governors *of the region* beyond the River, that they must permit me to pass through till I come to Judah, ⁸and a letter to Asaph the keeper of the king's forest, that he must give me timber to make beams for the gates of the citadel which *pertains* to the temple, for the city wall, and for the house that I will occupy." And the king granted *them* to me according to the good hand of my God upon me.

⁹Then I went to the governors *in the region* beyond the River, and gave them the king's letters. Now the king had sent captains of the army and horsemen with me. ¹⁰When Sanballat the Horonite and Tobiah the Ammonite official heard *of it,* they were deeply disturbed that a man had come to seek the well-being of the children of Israel.

¹¹So I came to Jerusalem and was there three days. ¹²Then I arose in the night, I and a few men with me; I told no one what my God had

NCV

¹³I went out at night through the Valley Gate. I rode toward the Dragon Well and the Trash Gate, inspecting the walls of Jerusalem that had been broken down and the gates that had been destroyed by fire. ¹⁴Then I rode on toward the Fountain Gate and the King's Pool, but there was not enough room for the animal I was riding to pass through. ¹⁵So I went up the valley at night, inspecting the wall. Finally, I turned and went back in through the Valley Gate. ¹⁶The guards did not know where I had gone or what I was doing. I had not yet said anything to the Jewish people, the priests, the important men, the officers, or any of the others who would do the work.

¹⁷Then I said to them, "You can see the trouble we have here. Jerusalem is a pile of ruins, and its gates have been burned. Come, let's rebuild the wall of Jerusalem so we won't be full of shame any longer." ¹⁸I also told them how God had been kind to me and what the king had said to me.

Then they answered, "Let's start rebuilding." So they began to work hard.

¹⁹But when Sanballat the Horonite, Tobiah the Ammonite officer, and Geshem the Arab heard about it, they made fun of us and laughed at us. They said, "What are you doing? Are you turning against the king?"

²⁰But I answered them, "The God of heaven will give us success. We, his servants, will start rebuilding, but you have no share, claim, or memorial in Jerusalem."

NKJV

put in my heart to do at Jerusalem; nor was there any animal with me, except the one on which I rode. ¹³And I went out by night through the Valley Gate to the Serpent Well and the Refuse Gate, and viewed the walls of Jerusalem which were broken down and its gates which were burned with fire. ¹⁴Then I went on to the Fountain Gate and to the King's Pool, but *there was* no room for the animal under me to pass. ¹⁵So I went up in the night by the valley, and viewed the wall; then I turned back and entered by the Valley Gate, and so returned. ¹⁶And the officials did not know where I had gone or what I had done; I had not yet told the Jews, the priests, the nobles, the officials, or the others who did the work.

¹⁷Then I said to them, "You see the distress that we *are* in, how Jerusalem *lies* waste, and its gates are burned with fire. Come and let us build the wall of Jerusalem, that we may no longer be a reproach." ¹⁸And I told them of the hand of my God which had been good upon me, and also of the king's words that he had spoken to me.

So they said, "Let us rise up and build." Then they set their hands to *this* good *work*.

¹⁹But when Sanballat the Horonite, Tobiah the Ammonite official, and Geshem the Arab heard *of it,* they laughed at us and despised us, and said, "What *is* this thing that you are doing? Will you rebel against the king?"

²⁰So I answered them, and said to them, "The God of heaven Himself will prosper us; therefore we His servants will arise and build, but you have no heritage or right or memorial in Jerusalem."

DISCOVERY

Explore the Bible reading by discussing these questions.

2. Why did it take courage for Nehemiah to face the king on behalf of his people?

_____

_____

_____

3. What fears and obstacles did Nehemiah overcome?

_____

_____

_____

4. How did Nehemiah handle his fears?

_____

_____

_____

5. List several ways God protected and provided for Nehemiah.

_____

_____

_____

6. Why did Nehemiah credit God, rather than the king, for the kindness shown to him?

_____

_____

_____

INSPIRATION

Here is an uplifting thought from *The Inspirational Bible*.

What does a child say when he is face to face with the neighborhood bully? "My brother is bigger than your brother." "My dad is stronger than your dad." Then adults get into the act. A bumper sticker sighted on a Los Angeles freeway read, "My lawyer is better than your lawyer."

What does a three-year-old do when he gets a knot in his shoelaces? He runs to Daddy. What does a five-year-old girl do when she falls and skins her knee? She cries to Mommy for comfort.

When faced with a problem, danger, difficulty or sadness, we naturally go to someone who is bigger, stronger, and more powerful. Just as a child wants to crawl up on Daddy's lap or have Mommy's arms wrapped around him, so we go to our heavenly Father. He is the fortress that protects us from attack, the refuge that grants us asylum from persecution, the safe harbor that shelters us from the storms of life.

(From *A Dad's Blessing*
by Smalley and Trent)

RESPONSE

Use these questions to share more deeply with each other.

7. What do you usually do when you feel overwhelmed by fear?

_____

_____

_____

8. What new insights about dealing with fear can you gain from this passage?

_____

_____

_____

9. In what ways can fear prevent us from doing what God wants?

_____

_____

_____

PRAYER

Father, you are our fortress, our refuge, our safe harbor. You are a faithful father, always soothing our hurts, caring for our needs, and guarding us from danger. Teach us to run to you whenever we feel scared, to trust you with our problems and pain, and to thank you daily for your presence and protection.

JOURNALING

Take a few moments to record your personal insights from this lesson.

What fears and anxieties do I need to release to God?

ADDITIONAL QUESTIONS

10. What steps can you take to improve the way you cope with anxiety?

_____

_____

_____

11. In what ways have the testimonies of others helped you trust God?

_____

_____

_____

12. Who can you tell about God's protection and provision for you?

_____

_____

_____

For more Bible passages on God's protection, see Deuteronomy 23:14; Joshua 24:17; 1 Samuel 30:23; Ezra 9:8–9; Psalm 32:7; 40:11; 41:1–3; 91:14; John 17:11–15; 2 Thessalonians 3:3.

To complete the Books of Ezra and Nehemiah during this twelve-part study, read Nehemiah 2:1—3:16.

LESSON NINE

PERSEVERANCE

REFLECTION

Begin your study by sharing thoughts on this question.

1. Think of a time when you felt like giving up on a project. What motivated you to stick with it?

_____

_____

_____

BIBLE READING

Read Nehemiah 4:1–23 from the NCV or the NKJV.

NCV

¹When Sanballat heard we were rebuilding the wall, he was very angry, even furious. He made fun of the Jewish people. ²He said to his friends and those with power in Samaria, "What are these weak Jews doing? Will they rebuild the wall? Will they offer sacrifices? Can they finish it in one day? Can they bring stones back to life from piles of trash and ashes?"

³Tobiah the Ammonite, who was next to Sanballat, said, "If a fox climbed up on the stone wall they are building, it would break it down."

NKJV

¹But it so happened, when Sanballat heard that we were rebuilding the wall, that he was furious and very indignant, and mocked the Jews. ²And he spoke before his brethren and the army of Samaria, and said, "What are these feeble Jews doing? Will they fortify themselves? Will they offer sacrifices? Will they complete it in a day? Will they revive the stones from the heaps of rubbish—*stones* that are burned?"

³Now Tobiah the Ammonite *was* beside him, and he said, "Whatever they build, if even a fox

NCV

[4]I prayed, "Hear us, our God. We are hated. Turn the insults of Sanballat and Tobiah back on their own heads. Let them be captured and stolen like valuables. [5]Do not hide their guilt or take away their sins so that you can't see them, because they have insulted the builders."

[6]So we rebuilt the wall to half its height, because the people were willing to work.

[7]But Sanballat, Tobiah, the Arabs, the Ammonites, and the people from Ashdod were very angry when they heard that the repairs to Jerusalem's walls were continuing and that the holes in the wall were being closed. [8]So they all made plans to come to Jerusalem and fight and stir up trouble. [9]But we prayed to our God and appointed guards to watch for them day and night.

[10]The people of Judah said, "The workers are getting tired. There is so much trash we cannot rebuild the wall."

[11]And our enemies said, "The Jews won't know or see anything until we come among them and kill them and stop the work."

[12]Then the Jewish people who lived near our enemies came and told us ten times, "Everywhere you turn, the enemy will attack us."[13]So I put people behind the lowest places along the wall—the open places—and I put families together with their swords, spears, and bows. [14]Then I looked around and stood up and said to the important men, the leaders, and the rest of the people: "Don't be afraid of them. Remember the Lord, who is great and powerful. Fight for your brothers, your sons and daughters, your wives, and your homes."

[15]Then our enemies heard that we knew

NKJV

goes up *on it,* he will break down their stone wall."

[4]Hear, O our God, for we are despised; turn their reproach on their own heads, and give them as plunder to a land of captivity! [5]Do not cover their iniquity, and do not let their sin be blotted out from before You; for they have provoked *You* to anger before the builders.

[6]So we built the wall, and the entire wall was joined together up to half its *height,* for the people had a mind to work.

[7]Now it happened, when Sanballat, Tobiah, the Arabs, the Ammonites, and the Ashdodites heard that the walls of Jerusalem were being restored and the gaps were beginning to be closed, that they became very angry, [8]and all of them conspired together to come *and* attack Jerusalem and create confusion. [9]Nevertheless we made our prayer to our God, and because of them we set a watch against them day and night.

[10]Then Judah said, "The strength of the laborers is failing, and *there is* so much rubbish that we are not able to build the wall."

[11]And our adversaries said, "They will neither know nor see anything, till we come into their midst and kill them and cause the work to cease."

[12]So it was, when the Jews who dwelt near them came, that they told us ten times, "From whatever place you turn, *they will be* upon us."

[13]Therefore I positioned *men* behind the lower parts of the wall, at the openings; and I set the people according to their families, with their swords, their spears, and their bows. [14]And I looked, and arose and said to the

about their plans and that God had ruined their plans. So we all went back to the wall, each to his own work.

[16]From that day on, half my people worked on the wall. The other half was ready with spears, shields, bows, and armor. The officers stood in back of the people of Judah [17]who were building the wall. Those who carried materials did their work with one hand and carried a weapon with the other. [18]Each builder wore his sword at his side as he worked. The man who blew the trumpet to warn the people stayed next to me.

[19]Then I said to the important men, the leaders, and the rest of the people, "This is a very big job. We are spreading out along the wall so that we are far apart. [20]Wherever you hear the sound of the trumpet, assemble there. Our God will fight for us."

[21]So we continued to work with half the men holding spears from sunrise till the stars came out. [22]At that time I also said to the people, "Let every man and his helper stay inside Jerusalem at night. They can be our guards at night and workmen during the day." [23]Neither I, my brothers, my workers, nor the guards with me ever took off our clothes. Each person carried his weapon even when he went for water.

nobles, to the leaders, and to the rest of the people, "Do not be afraid of them. Remember the Lord, great and awesome, and fight for your brethren, your sons, your daughters, your wives, and your houses."

[15]And it happened, when our enemies heard that it was known to us, and *that* God had brought their plot to nothing, that all of us returned to the wall, everyone to his work. [16]So it was, from that time on, *that* half of my servants worked at construction, while the other half held the spears, the shields, the bows, and *wore* armor; and the leaders *were* behind all the house of Judah. [17]Those who built on the wall, and those who carried burdens, loaded themselves so that with one hand they worked at construction, and with the other held a weapon. [18]Every one of the builders had his sword girded at his side as he built. And the one who sounded the trumpet *was* beside me.

[19]Then I said to the nobles, the rulers, and the rest of the people, "The work *is* great and extensive, and we are separated far from one another on the wall. [20]"Wherever you hear the sound of the trumpet, rally to us there. Our God will fight for us."

[21]So we labored in the work, and half of *the men* held the spears from daybreak until the stars appeared. [22]At the same time I also said to the people, "Let each man and his servant stay at night in Jerusalem, that they may be our guard by night and a working party by day." [23]So neither I, my brethren, my servants, nor the men of the guard who followed me took off our clothes, *except* that everyone took them off for washing.

DISCOVERY

Explore the Bible reading by discussing these questions.

2. Describe the opposition the Jews encountered to their building project.

_____

_____

_____

3. How did Nehemiah respond to the ridicule and threats of others?

_____

_____

_____

4. What do you think gave the Jews the strength to carry on, despite persecution and danger?

_____

_____

_____

5. What was the wisdom of the plan that Nehemiah devised to accomplish the task of rebuilding the wall?

_____

_____

_____

6. What leadership skills do you see in Nehemiah?

_____

_____

_____

INSPIRATION

Here is an uplifting thought from *The Inspirational Bible.*

Bart decided to ask God to shape his character. He surrendered his own will to the will of God. At the time, Bart's business floundered on the verge of failure. "Should I throw in the towel, or keep trying to hang on?" Bart wondered.

God replies, "You need to persevere." After we have done the will of God, then we will receive our reward. God's will is for us to demonstrate to a hurting world how wonderfully His power can work within the person who perseveres.

Certainly, there are days when we feel like we will die, or maybe even wish we could, but we keep going. Why? Why do we keep going? Because *when* we have done the will of God we *will* receive what He has promised.

Will persevering guarantee we will succeed in the worldly sense of success? Is that what He has promised? Does it mean we will not go out of business if we hang on? No, but we can state emphatically that if we don't persevere we will not succeed in any sense. Not persevering guarantees we will fail. . . .

Beyond succeeding in a worldly sense, though God wants our character to succeed more than our circumstances to succeed. He will adjust our circumstances in such a way that our character eventually succeeds, for that is His highest aim, His will.

(From *Walking with Christ in the Details of Life* by Patrick Morley)

RESPONSE

Use these questions to share more deeply with each other.

7. Which of Nehemiah's character traits would you like to cultivate in your own life?

_____

_____

_____

8. List some rewards of perseverance.

_____

_____

_____

9. Think of a time when you had to persevere through discouragement, fatigue, or pressure. What helped you do that?

_____

_____

_____

PRAYER

Father, we know that you allow us to experience troubles because you want to strengthen our character. So we ask you to help us view our problems as opportunities to learn and grow. In the face of opposition, pressure, or pain, help us to stand firm. May our lives be models of faithfulness and perseverance until the day of Christ's return.

JOURNALING

Take a few moments to record your personal insights from this lesson.

What situation in my life is helping me to develop perseverance?

ADDITIONAL QUESTIONS

10. Why is it important for believers to model perseverance?

_____

_____

_____

11. In what ways can we combat feelings of discouragement and hopelessness?

_____

_____

_____

12. How can you encourage a friend who may feel like giving up?

_____

_____

_____

For more Bible passages on perseverance, see Luke 8:15; 1 Timothy 4:16; Hebrews 10:35–36; 12:1–3; James 1:3–4, 12; 5:11; Revelation 2:2–3.

To complete the Books of Ezra and Nehemiah during this twelve-part study, read Nehemiah 3:17—4:23.

LESSON TEN

GOD HELPS THE HURTING

REFLECTION

Begin your study by sharing thoughts on this question.

1. Think of someone who reached out to you when you were hurting. Describe what that person's support meant to you.

_____

_____

_____

BIBLE READING

Read Nehemiah 5:1–13 from the NCV or the NKJV.

NCV

¹The men and their wives complained loudly against their fellow Jews. ²Some of them were saying, "We have many sons and daughters in our families. To eat and stay alive, we need grain."

³Others were saying, "We are borrowing money against our fields, vineyards, and homes to get grain because there is not much food."

⁴And still others were saying, "We are

NKJV

¹And there was a great outcry of the people and their wives against their Jewish brethren. ²For there were those who said, "We, our sons, and our daughters *are* many; therefore let us get grain, that we may eat and live."

³There were also *some* who said, "We have mortgaged our lands and vineyards and houses, that we might buy grain because of the famine."

⁴There were also those who said, "We have

borrowing money to pay the king's tax on our fields and vineyards. ⁵We are just like our fellow Jews, and our sons are like their sons. But we have to sell our sons and daughters as slaves. Some of our daughters have already been sold. But there is nothing we can do, because our fields and vineyards already belong to other people."

⁶When I heard their complaints about these things, I was very angry. ⁷After I thought about it, I accused the important people and the leaders, "You are charging your own brothers too much interest." So I called a large meeting to deal with them. ⁸I said to them, "As much as possible, we have bought freedom for our fellow Jews who had been sold to foreigners. Now you are selling your fellow Jews to us!" The leaders were quiet and had nothing to say.

⁹Then I said, "What you are doing is not right. Don't you fear God? Don't let our foreign enemies shame us. ¹⁰I, my brothers, and my men are also lending money and grain to the people. But stop charging them so much for this. ¹¹Give back their fields, vineyards, olive trees, and houses right now. Also give back the extra amount you charged—the hundredth part of the money, grain, new wine, and oil."

¹²They said, "We will give it back and not demand anything more from them. We will do as you say."

Then I called for the priests, and I made the important men and leaders take an oath to do what they had said. ¹³Also I shook out the folds of my robe and said, "In this way may God shake out everyone who does not keep his promise. May God shake him out of his house

borrowed money for the king's tax *on* our lands and vineyards. ⁵Yet now our flesh *is* as the flesh of our brethren, our children as their children; and indeed we are forcing our sons and our daughters to be slaves, and *some* of our daughters have been brought into slavery. *It is* not in our power *to redeem them,* for other men have our lands and vineyards."

⁶And I became very angry when I heard their outcry and these words. ⁷After serious thought, I rebuked the nobles and rulers, and said to them, "Each of you is exacting usury from his brother." So I called a great assembly against them. ⁸And I said to them, "According to our ability we have redeemed our Jewish brethren who were sold to the nations. Now indeed, will you even sell your brethren? Or should they be sold to us?"

Then they were silenced and found nothing *to say.* ⁹Then I said, "What you are doing *is* not good. Should you not walk in the fear of our God because of the reproach of the nations, our enemies? ¹⁰I also, *with* my brethren and my servants, am lending them money and grain. Please, let us stop this usury! ¹¹Restore now to them, even this day, their lands, their vineyards, their olive groves, and their houses, also a hundredth of the money and the grain, the new wine and the oil, that you have charged them."

¹²So they said, "We will restore *it,* and will require nothing from them; we will do as you say."

Then I called the priests, and required an oath from them that they would do according to this promise. ¹³Then I shook out the fold of my garment and said, "So may God shake out

NCV	NKJV
and out of the things that are his. Let that person be shaken out and emptied!" Then the whole group said, "Amen," and they praised the LORD. So the people did what they had promised.	each man from his house, and from his property, who does not perform this promise. Even thus may he be shaken out and emptied." And all the assembly said, "Amen!" and praised the LORD. Then the people did according to this promise.

DISCOVERY

Explore the Bible reading by discussing these questions.

2. Describe the condition of many of the returned exiles.

_____

_____

_____

3. How did Nehemiah come to the defense of his fellow Jews?

_____

_____

_____

4. In what ways did some of the rich, influential Jews take advantage of their own people?

_____

_____

_____

5. According to Nehemiah, people who fear God should treat the poor with kindness and deference. How does that compare to today's world?

_____

_____

_____

6. Why do you think Nehemiah had the boldness to take a stand against the leaders the way he did?

_____

_____

_____

INSPIRATION

Here is an uplifting thought from *The Inspirational Bible.*

Why do I not take him seriously when he questions, "If you, then, though you are evil, know how to give good gifts to your children, how much more will your Father in Heaven give good gifts to those who ask him!"

Why don't I let my Father do for me what I am more than willing to do for my own children?

I'm learning, though. Being a parent is better than a course on theology. Being a father is teaching me that when I am criticized, injured, or afraid, there is a Father who is ready to comfort me. There is a Father who will hold me until I'm better, help me until I can live with the hurt, and who won't go to sleep when I'm afraid of waking up and seeing the dark. Ever. And that's enough.

(From *The Applause of Heaven* by Max Lucado)

RESPONSE

Use these questions to share more deeply with each other.

7. In what ways is God's concern for hurting people revealed in this passage?

_____

_____

_____

8. Why do we sometimes doubt God's willingness or ability to help us?

_____

_____

_____

9. Share an example of how God has met a physical, emotional, or financial need in your life.

_____

_____

_____

PRAYER

Father, we're grateful that you are concerned about the needs of people. You comfort the hurting, care for the needy, provide for the poor, and deliver the oppressed. Because we trust you, Father, we bring our needs to you and ask you to work in our hearts. Heal our wounds, so that we may become vessels of your love pouring out to others.

JOURNALING

Take a few moments to record your personal insights from this lesson.

What wounds in my life do I need to ask God to heal?

ADDITIONAL QUESTIONS

10. In what ways can you express your appreciation to God for his care for you?

_____

_____

_____

11. What responsibility do you have to help the poor and oppressed?

_____

_____

_____

12. Who is one hurting person you can reach with God's love this week?

_____

_____

_____

For more Bible passages on God's care for people, see Psalm 8:4–5; 98:3; Isaiah 49:15–17; Matthew 6:26–32; Luke 12:6–7; 1 Peter 5:7.

To complete the Books of Ezra and Nehemiah during this twelve-part study, read Nehemiah 5:1—7:73.

LESSON ELEVEN

GOD'S LOVE AND FAITHFULNESS

REFLECTION

Begin your study by sharing thoughts on this question.

1. Describe a time when you felt God's love in a tangible way.

_____

_____

_____

BIBLE READING

Read Nehemiah 9:5–21 from the NCV or the NKJV.

NCV	NKJV
⁵Then these Levites spoke: Jeshua, Kadmiel, Bani, Hashabneiah, Sherebiah, Hodiah, Shebaniah, and Pethahiah. They said, "Stand up and praise the LORD your God, who lives forever and ever."	⁵And the Levites, Jeshua, Kadmiel, Bani, Hashabniah, Sherebiah, Hodijah, Shebaniah, *and* Pethahiah, said:

"Blessed be your wonderful name.
    It is more wonderful than all blessing
        and praise.
⁶ You are the only LORD.
    You made the heavens, even the
        highest heavens,
    with all the stars.
	¹ "Stand up *and* bless the LORD your God
	    Forever and ever!
	
	"Blessed be Your glorious name,
	    Which is exalted above all blessing and
	        praise!
	⁶ You alone *are* the LORD;
	    You have made heaven,

NCV

You made the earth and everything on it,
  the seas and everything in them;
  you give life to everything.
The heavenly army worships you.

7 "You are the LORD,
  the God who chose Abram
and brought him out of Ur in Babylonia
  and named him Abraham.
8 You found him faithful to you,
  so you made an agreement with him
to give his descendants the land of the
    Canaanites,
  Hittites, Amorites,
  Perizzites, Jebusites, and Girgashites.
You have kept your promise,
  because you do what is right.

9 "You saw our ancestors suffering in Egypt
  and heard them cry out at the Red Sea.
10 You did signs and miracles against the
    king of Egypt,
  and against all his officers and all his
    people,
  because you knew how proud they
    were.
You became as famous as you are today.
11 You divided the sea in front of our
    ancestors;
  they walked through on dry ground.
But you threw the people chasing them
    into the deep water,
  like a stone thrown into mighty waters.
12 You led our ancestors with a pillar of
    cloud by day
  and with a pillar of fire at night.

NKJV

The heaven of heavens, with all their host,
The earth and everything on it,
The seas and all that is in them,
And You preserve them all.
The host of heaven worships You.

7 "You *are* the LORD God,
  Who chose Abram,
  And brought him out of Ur of the
    Chaldeans,
  And gave him the name Abraham;
8 You found his heart faithful before You,
  And made a covenant with him
  To give the land of the Canaanites,
  The Hittites, the Amorites,
  the Perizzites, the Jebusites,
  And the Girgashites—
  To give *it* to his descendants.
  You have performed Your words,
  For You *are* righteous.

9 "You saw the affliction of our fathers in
    Egypt,
  And heard their cry by the Red Sea.
10 You showed signs and wonders against
    Pharaoh,
  Against all his servants,
  And against all the people of his land.
  For You knew that they acted proudly
    against them.
  So You made a name for Yourself, as *it is*
    this day.
11 And You divided the sea before them,
  So that they went through the midst of the
    sea on the dry land;

NCV

It lit the way
 they were supposed to go.
¹³ You came down to Mount Sinai
 and spoke from heaven to our ancestors.
You gave them fair rules and true
 teachings,
 good orders and commands.
¹⁴ You told them about your holy Sabbath
 and gave them commands, orders, and
 teachings
 through your servant Moses.
¹⁵ When they were hungry, you gave them
 bread from heaven.
 When they were thirsty, you brought
 them water from the rock.
You told them to enter and take over
 the land you had promised to give
 them.

¹⁶ "But our ancestors were proud and
 stubborn
 and did not obey your commands.
¹⁷ They refused to listen;
 they forgot the miracles you did for
 them.
So they became stubborn and turned
 against you,
 choosing a leader to take them back to
 slavery.
But you are a forgiving God.
 You are kind and full of mercy.
You do not become angry quickly, and
 you have great love.
 So you did not leave them.
¹⁸ Our ancestors even made an idol of a calf
 for themselves.

NKJV

And their persecutors You threw into the
 deep,
 As a stone into the mighty waters.
¹² Moreover You led them by day with a cloudy
 pillar,
 And by night with a pillar of fire,
 To give them light on the road
 Which they should travel.

¹³ "You came down also on Mount Sinai,
 And spoke with them from heaven,
 And gave them just ordinances and true
 laws,
 Good statutes and commandments.
¹⁴ You made known to them Your holy
 Sabbath,
 And commanded them precepts, statutes
 and laws,
 By the hand of Moses Your servant.
¹⁵ You gave them bread from heaven for their
 hunger,
 And brought them water out of the rock
 for their thirst,
 And told them to go in to possess the land
 Which You had sworn to give them.

¹⁶ "But they and our fathers acted proudly,
 Hardened their necks,
 And did not heed Your commandments.
¹⁷ They refused to obey,
 And they were not mindful of Your
 wonders
 That You did among them.
 But they hardened their necks,
 And in their rebellion
 They appointed a leader

NCV

They said, 'This is your god, Israel,
who brought you up out of Egypt.'
They spoke against you.

19 "You have great mercy,
so you did not leave them in the desert.
The pillar of cloud guided them by day,
and the pillar of fire led them at night,
lighting the way they were to go.
20 You gave your good Spirit to teach them.
You gave them manna to eat
and water when they were thirsty.
21 You took care of them for forty years in
the desert;
they needed nothing.
Their clothes did not wear out,
and their feet did not swell.

NKJV

To return to their bondage.
But You *are* God,
Ready to pardon,
Gracious and merciful,
Slow to anger,
Abundant in kindness,
And did not forsake them.

18 "Even when they made a molded calf for
themselves,
And said, 'This *is* your god
That brought you up out of Egypt,'
And worked great provocations,
19 Yet in Your manifold mercies
You did not forsake them in the
wilderness.
The pillar of the cloud did not depart
from them by day,
To lead them on the road;
Nor the pillar of fire by night,
To show them light,
And the way they should go.
20 You also gave Your good Spirit to instruct
them,
And did not withhold Your manna from
their mouth,
And gave them water for their thirst.
21 Forty years You sustained them in the
wilderness,
They lacked nothing;
Their clothes did not wear out
And their feet did not swell.

DISCOVERY

Explore the Bible reading by discussing these questions.

2. List some of the ways God displayed his love for the people of Israel.

_____

_____

_____

3. Why did the Israelites break their covenant with God after he had provided for them so graciously?

_____

_____

_____

4. How did God repay his people for their unfaithfulness?

_____

_____

_____

5. Which of God's attributes did the Levites highlight in their prayer?

_____

_____

_____

6. What was the benefit to Israel for their leaders to summarize the history of God's provision?

_____

_____

_____

INSPIRATION

Here is an uplifting thought from *The Inspirational Bible*.

Some time ago Denalyn [my wife] was gone for a couple of days and left me alone with the girls. Though the time was not without the typical children's quarrels and occasional misbehavior, it went fine.

"How were the girls?" Denalyn asked when she got home.

"Good. No problem at all."

Jenna overheard my response. "We weren't good, Daddy," she objected. "We fought once, we didn't do what you said once. We weren't good. How can you say we were good?"

Jenna and I had different perceptions of what pleases a father. She thought it depended upon what she did. It didn't. We think the same about God. We think his love rises and falls with our performance. It doesn't. I don't love Jenna for what she does. I love her for whose she is. She is mine.

God loves you for the same reason. He loves you for whose you are, you are his child. It was this love that pursued the Israelites. It was this love that sent the prophets. It was this love which wrapped itself in human flesh and descended the birth canal of Mary. It was this love which walked the hard trails of Galilee and spoke to the hard hearts of the religious.

"This is not normal, Lord God," David exclaimed as he considered God's love. You are right, David. God's love is not normal love. It's not normal to love a murderer and adulterer, but God did when he loved David. It isn't normal to love a man who takes his eyes off you, but such was God's love for Solomon. It isn't normal to love people who love stone idols more than they love you, but God did when he refused to give up on Israel.

(From *And the Angels Were Silent*
by Max Lucado)

RESPONSE

Use these questions to share more deeply with each other.

7. In what ways is God's love different than human love?

_____

_____

_____

8. List some common misconceptions we have about the way God relates to us.

_____

_____

_____

9. In what ways does this passage encourage you to trust God?

_____

_____

_____

PRAYER

Father, thank you for pursuing us with an everlasting love. Thank you for making us your children and loving us as your own. We praise you for your faithfulness and trustworthiness. Deepen our understanding of your love, and help us to remain faithful to you.

JOURNALING

Take a few moments to record your personal insights from this lesson.

When can I set aside some time to meditate on God's love and faithfulness?

ADDITIONAL QUESTIONS

10. What are the benefits of remembering God's past works?

_____

_____

_____

11. What happens when we ignore or forget what God has done for us?

_____

_____

_____

12. How do you respond to knowing that God will love you and remain faithful to you, no matter how often you fail him?

_____

_____

_____

For more Bible passages on God's love, see Deuteronomy 7:8–9; Jeremiah 31:3; John 3:16; Romans 5:8; Ephesians 2:4–5; 1 John 3:1; 4:7–19.

To complete the Books of Ezra and Nehemiah during this twelve-part study, read Nehemiah 8:1—10:27.

ADDITIONAL THOUGHTS

LESSON TWELVE

GIVING TO THE CHURCH

REFLECTION

Begin your study by sharing thoughts on this idea.

1. Describe a time when someone gave you the very best they had to offer.

_____

_____

_____

BIBLE READING

Read Nehemiah 10:28–39 from the NCV or the NKJV.

NCV

[28]The rest of the people took an oath. They were the priests, Levites, gatekeepers, singers, Temple servants, all those who separated themselves from foreigners to keep the Teachings of God, and also their wives and their sons and daughters who could understand. [29]They joined their fellow Israelites and their leading men in taking an oath, which was tied to a curse in case they broke the oath. They promised to follow the Teachings of God, which they had been given through Moses the servant of

NKJV

[28]Now the rest of the people—the priests, the Levites, the gatekeepers, the singers, the Nethinim, and all those who had separated themselves from the peoples of the lands to the Law of God, their wives, their sons, and their daughters, everyone who had knowledge and understanding—[29]these joined with their brethren, their nobles, and entered into a curse and an oath to walk in God's Law, which was given by Moses the servant of God, and to observe and do all the commandments of the

NCV

God, and to obey all the commands, rules, and laws of the LORD our God.

[30]They said:

We promise not to let our daughters marry foreigners nor to let our sons marry their daughters. [31]Foreigners may bring goods or grain to sell on the Sabbath, but we will not buy on the Sabbath or any holy day. Every seventh year we will not plant, and that year we will forget all that people owe us.

[32]We will be responsible for the commands to pay for the service of the Temple of our God. We will give an eighth of an ounce of silver each year. [33]It is for the bread that is set out on the table; the regular grain offerings and burnt offerings; the offerings on the Sabbaths, New Moon festivals, and special feasts; the holy offerings; the offerings to remove the sins of the Israelites so they will belong to God; and for the work of the Temple of our God.

[34]We, the priests, the Levites, and the people, have thrown lots to decide at what time of year each family must bring wood to the Temple. The wood is for burning on the altar of the LORD our God, and we will do this as it is written in the Teachings.

[35]We also will bring the first fruits from our crops and the first fruits of every tree to the Temple each year.

[36]We will bring to the Temple our first-born sons and cattle and the firstborn of our herds and flocks, as it is written in the Teachings. We will bring them to the priests who are serving in the Temple.

NKJV

LORD our Lord, and His ordinances and His statutes: [30]We would not give our daughters as wives to the peoples of the land, nor take their daughters for our sons; [31]if the peoples of the land brought wares or any grain to sell on the Sabbath day, we would not buy it from them on the Sabbath, or on a holy day; and we would forego the seventh year's *produce* and the exacting of every debt.

[32]Also we made ordinances for ourselves, to exact from ourselves yearly one-third of a shekel for the service of the house of our God: [33]for the showbread, for the regular grain offering, for the regular burnt offering of the Sabbaths, the New Moons, and the set feasts; for the holy things, for the sin offerings to make atonement for Israel, and all the work of the house of our God. [34]We cast lots among the priests, the Levites, and the people, for *bringing* the wood offering into the house of our God, according to our fathers' houses, at the appointed times year by year, to burn on the altar of the LORD our God as *it is* written in the Law.

[35]And *we made ordinances* to bring the firstfruits of our ground and the firstfruits of all fruit of all trees, year by year, to the house of the LORD; [36]to bring the firstborn of our sons and our cattle, as *it is* written in the Law, and the firstborn of our herds and our flocks, to the house of our God, to the priests who minister in the house of our God; [37]to bring the firstfruits of our dough, our offerings, the fruit from all kinds of trees, *the* new wine and oil, to the priests, to the storerooms of the house of our God; and to bring the tithes of our land to the

NCV

³⁷We will bring to the priests at the store-rooms of the Temple the first of our ground meal, our offerings, the fruit from all our trees, and our new wine and oil. And we will bring a tenth of our crops to the Levites, who will collect these things in all the towns where we work. ³⁸A priest of Aaron's family must be with the Levites when they receive the tenth of the people's crops. The Levites must bring a tenth of all they receive to the Temple of our God to put in the storerooms of the treasury. ³⁹The people of Israel and the Levites are to bring to the storerooms the gifts of grain, new wine, and oil. That is where the utensils for the Temple are kept and where the priests who are serving, the gatekeepers, and singers stay.

We will not ignore the Temple of our God.

NKJV

Levites, for the Levites should receive the tithes in all our farming communities. ³⁸And the priest, the descendant of Aaron, shall be with the Levites when the Levites receive tithes; and the Levites shall bring up a tenth of the tithes to the house of our God, to the rooms of the storehouse.

³⁹For the children of Israel and the children of Levi shall bring the offering of the grain, of the new wine and the oil, to the storerooms where the articles of the sanctuary *are, where* the priests who minister and the gatekeepers and the singers *are;* and we will not neglect the house of our God.

DISCOVERY

Explore the Bible reading by discussing these questions.

2. How did the Israelites renew their covenant with God?

_____

_____

_____

3. What areas of life were affected by their agreement with God?

_____

_____

_____

4. In what concrete ways did the people plan to show their devotion to God?

_____

_____

_____

5. What specifications did the people make about their gifts to the Temple?

_____

_____

_____

6. Why does God desire the first and best of people's resources?

_____

_____

_____

INSPIRATION

Here is an uplifting thought from *The Inspirational Bible*.

You don't give for God's sake. You give for your sake. "The purpose of tithing is to teach you to always put God first in your lives" (Deut. 14:23 TLB). How does tithing teach you? Consider the simple act of writing a check for the offering. First you enter the date. Already you are reminded that you are a time-bound creature and every possession you have will rust or burn. Best to give it while you can.

Then you enter the name of the one to whom you are giving the money. If the bank would cash it, you'd write *God*. But they won't, so you write the name of the church or group that has earned your trust.

Next comes the amount. Ahh, the moment of truth. You're more than a person with a checkbook. You're David, placing a stone in the sling. You're Peter, one foot on the boat, one foot on the lake. You're a little boy in a big crowd. A picnic lunch is all the Teacher needs, but it's all you have.

What will you do? Sling the Stone? Take the Step? Give the Meal?

Careful now, don't move too quickly. You aren't just entering an amount . . . you are making a confession. A confession that God owns it all anyway.

And then the line in the lower left-hand corner on which you write what the check is for. Hard to know what to put. It's for the light bills and literature. A little bit of outreach. A little bit of salary.

Better yet, it's partial payment for what the church has done to help you raise your family . . . keep your own priorities sorted out . . . tune you in to his ever-nearness.

Or, perhaps, best yet, it's for you. It's a moment for you to clip yet another strand from the rope of earth so that when he returns you won't be tied up.

(From *When God Whispers Your Name* by Max Lucado)

RESPONSE

Use these questions to share more deeply with each other.

7. What principles from Israel's covenant with God are applicable to us today?

_____

_____

_____

8. Explain the importance to you of tithing.

_____

_____

_____

9. What do we receive in return when we give money to the church?

_____

_____

_____

PRAYER

Father, you deserve the best we can give because all we have comes from your gracious hand. Forgive us for clinging to our possessions, our time, and our money. Help us to see the importance of giving you the first fruits of our labors. Teach us what it means to make you the Lord of our lives.

JOURNALING

Take a few moments to record your personal insights from this lesson.

When am I tempted to hold back my best from God?

ADDITIONAL QUESTIONS

10. What is the connection between tithing and worship?

_____

_____

_____

11. In what ways can money enslave people?

_____

_____

_____

12. What steps can you take to loosen your grip on your financial resources?

_____

_____

_____

For more Bible passages on giving, see Leviticus 27:30; Deuteronomy 14:22–28; Matthew 6:3–4; 22:21; Acts 20:35; 1 Corinthians 16:1–2; 2 Corinthians 9:7–8.

To complete the Books of Ezra and Nehemiah during this twelve-part study, read Nehemiah 10:28—13:31.

ADDITIONAL THOUGHTS

ADDITIONAL THOUGHTS

LEADERS' NOTES

LESSON ONE

Question 2: God is the God of all the world and all of history. Throughout Scripture, we see God working through rulers and world events to bring about his purpose. He hardened Pharaoh's heart towards Moses and the Israelites, resulting in the miracles of Exodus. He caused the decree of Caesar Augustus that brought Joseph and Mary to Bethlehem to fulfill the prophecy of the Messiah's birthplace. Romans 13:1 tells us that every authority that exists has been established by God. Our God is in charge of it all!

Question 12: God never gives us more than we can handle. If he asks us to do something, he'll give us all we need to accomplish it. Second Peter 1:3 says that God has given us everything we need for life and godliness. First Corinthians 10:13 reminds us God will always provide a way out of temptation in order that we might obey him. If God is calling you to do something, you can be sure that you have all the resources necessary to do it.

LESSON TWO

Question 5: For further discussion, talk about this issue in light of today. In what ways is it important for us to demonstrate publicly our faith in God? What difference does this make in our workplaces, communities, or families?

Question 11: Group members can learn more of what God has to say about fear and boldness by looking at Psalm 56:3–4, Acts 4:29, Romans 1:16, Romans 8:15, and 2 Timothy 1:7–8.

LESSON THREE

Question 5: Encourage the group to think through what this meant for the Jews, and why it was so important that they do it. Part of God's original purpose in giving them the law in Leviticus was to make them different than the nations surrounding them. Why did God do this, and how does it relate to the actions of the Israelites who returned from captivity?

Question 10: Group members may not be able to identify a "spectacular" way in which God has provided for them. Encourage them to broaden their definition of spectacular to include things they might otherwise take for granted: the way God provided a spouse or children, their salvation or the salvation of a friend or family member, a job with a steady paycheck, finding a church family to worship with. God's daily faithfulness in these areas, and thousands more that we tend to overlook is indeed spectacular.

LESSON FOUR

Question 4: We see that Ezra was concerned with upholding God's reputation. This is a common theme throughout the Bible. In what ways does the church today show its concern for God's reputation among those outside the church? In what ways does the church show a lack of concern? What can we learn from Ezra in regard to this?

Question 12: You may want to ask if anyone in the group is currently in a situation where it's tempting to trust their own resources rather than God. This is the person who needs extra encouragement to remember God's care for them in the past. Spend some time as a group praying for each person who shares their needs.

LESSON FIVE

Question 5: In Daniel 9, Daniel, like Ezra, includes himself in his prayer of repentance, though he had been faithful to God. What can we learn from the example of these men? What sense of responsibility should we feel for the sins of the church today? How can this influence our attitudes, our actions, and our prayers?

Question 12: This question requires group members to share openly and make themselves vulnerable. Be sensitive to this. Seek to draw out an honest answer from each member, but don't push anyone to share who is uncomfortable doing so. If the atmosphere of your group doesn't promote this kind of open sharing, think through ways you can help members feel more comfortable with one another. Perhaps you might want to plan some time before or after the group to share a cup of coffee and talk. Maybe you could have a potluck together. Look for ways to serve the members of your group, and encourage them to look for ways to serve each other. And pray for one another!

LESSON SIX

Question 8: Ezekiel 18:30–32 provides a good starting place for answering this question. True repentance involves turning away from sin, getting rid of the things in your life that relate to that sin, and getting a new heart and a new spirit. It implies that you are walking in one direction, then you make a U-turn and start walking in the opposite direction. The Israelites in Ezra are an excellent example of this. They had disobeyed God by marrying non-Jewish women, and they repented by separating themselves from them. They didn't just tell God they knew they were wrong, they demonstrated their change of heart through their actions.

Question 10: For more on sin's affect on your relationship with God and with others you can look at Psalm 66:18, Matthew 5:23–24, Mark 11:25, Romans 12:18, and Romans 14:19.

LESSON SEVEN

Question 3: Nehemiah's example is a challenge to us. Ask the group to consider this: If you were in Nehemiah's shoes, how would you have responded? If your response would have been prayer, what would you have prayed for? How would your prayer have differed from Nehemiah's?

Question 10: Philippians 4:6–7 says, "Do not worry about anything, but pray and ask God for everything you need, always giving thanks. And God's peace, which is so great we cannot understand it, will keep your hearts and your minds in Christ Jesus." Prayer may not always change our circumstances, but it always changes us. Through prayer, God grants us his peace to face any situation we are in.

LESSON EIGHT

Question 6: Nehemiah had an incredible awareness of God's control over all things. He saw God's hand working through the king, and he saw himself as nothing more than a tool that God was using to accomplish his purpose in Jerusalem. Have the group take a moment to compare themselves to Nehemiah in this area. You may want to ask them to consider some of the following questions: In what ways have you recognized God's kindness to you through another person? In what ways may you have failed to give God the credit due him? In what ways is God using you as a tool, and how are you doing at giving God the recognition he deserves in this?

Question 7: To prompt discussion, you can rephrase the question by asking for examples of what causes fear in the life of your group members. You may suggest such situations as giving a big presentation at work, taking an important test, a first date, making a presentation at school or church, being in a car accident, undergoing a surgical procedure, the birth of a child or signing a mortgage. Once you have identified fearful situations, ask what they do in response to their fear.

LESSON NINE

Question 3: Some in your group may be able to identify with Nehemiah. Are they facing a situation where they are ridiculed or threatened, especially because of their faith? First Peter has a lot to say on this subject. Encourage group members to read through the book on their own or look together at 1 Peter 2:19–24, 3:13–17, and 4:12–16.

Question 11: Whenever our emotions threaten to overwhelm us, we can look to the promises of God's Word to help keep our feelings in line. When we are discouraged or feel helpless, we can look at verses like Deuteronomy 31:8, Joshua 1:9, Psalm 42:5, Psalm 19:43,49,74,81,114,147, and Romans 15:4, 13.

LESSON TEN

Question 9: You may want to pause and spend a few minutes in prayer thanking God for what group members share in answer to this question. It's important that we praise and thank God for the ways he answers our prayers and blesses us!

Question 11: Spend some time as a group brainstorming how an individual or church in your community may help the poor and oppressed. Are there organizations you might get involved with or people you could contact for ideas? Does anyone already know a family or individual in need of help?

LESSON ELEVEN

Question 2: You can also take a look at Psalm 105 which recounts the history of Israel and highlights God's love and provision for the people of Israel. You may want to divide the Psalm among your group and have them read their portion and list the ways God displayed his love to Israel.

Question 8: Some examples of common misconceptions may include God as a kindly but inept grandfather, God as the genie in the bottle who grants our every wish, God as the police-man waiting to punish any wrong action, or God as a reflection of our own imperfect fathers.

Question 10: You may want to have group members spend some time writing down at least twenty ways God has demonstrated his love and provision for them. Being forced to recall this many items will encourage them to see God's hand in things they might otherwise overlook or have forgotten about.

LESSON TWELVE

Question 3: The Israelites's agreement affected them in every area of life—family life, economically, socially, spiritually. Often, we try to "give God" certain areas of our lives, while doing whatever we want in the other areas. Ask what areas of life your group members hold back from God.

Question 12: It helps to remember that what we think of as *our* financial resources don't really belong to us. Everything that we have is loaned to us by God, and he gives it to us to use in ways that please him. Ask for examples of how we handle our money differently when we treat it as if it belongs to God. You may want to read Luke 12:33–34: "Get for yourselves purses that will not wear out, the treasure in heaven that never runs out, where thieves can't steal and moths can't destroy. Your heart will be where your treasure is."

ADDITIONAL NOTES

ACKNOWLEDGMENTS

Lucado, Max. *And the Angels Were Silent*, Questar Publishers, Multnomah Books, copyright 1992 by Max Lucado.

Lucado, Max. *God Came Near*, Questar Publishers, Multnomah Books, copyright 1987.

Lucado, Max. *He Still Moves Stones*, copyright 1993, Word Inc., Dallas, Texas.

Lucado, Max. *In the Eye of the Storm*, copyright 1991, Word Inc., Dallas, Texas.

Lucado, Max. *On the Anvil*, copyright 1985 by Max Lucado. Used by permission of Tyndale House Publishers, Inc. All rights reserved.

Lucado, Max. *The Applause of Heaven*, copyright 1990, Word Inc., Dallas, Texas.

Lucado, Max. *When God Whispers Your Name*, copyright 1994, Word Inc., Dallas, Texas.

Morley, Patrick. *Walking with Christ in the Details of Life*, copyright 1992 Thomas Nelson, Nashville, Tennessee.

Smalley, Gary and Trent, John. *A Dad's Blessing*, copyright 1994 Thomas Nelson, Nashville, Tennessee.

Swindoll, Charles. *Hand Me Another Brick*, copyright 1990 Thomas Nelson, Nashville, Tennessee.